MW01241372

The Zane Grey Primer

Selections by Zane Grey

Compiled by Ed Meyer

for Zane Grey's West Society

A Publication of Zane Grey's West Society

www.zgws.org

The Zane Grey Primer
Compiled by Ed Meyer for Zane Grey's West Society

Library of Congress
Cataloging-in-Publication Data
Zane Grey's West Society
The Zane Grey Primer

ISBN-13: 978-1523274857

Cover art adapted from a photo provided courtesy of Barry Glazier.

Zane Grey's West Society
www.zgws.org

THE ZANE GREY PRIMER

Other Zane Grey's West Society Publications

Riders of the Purple Sage—Centennial Edition (2012)
Hard cover and paperback

The Young Forester (2015)
Paperback

To order these books or other items,

visit the ZGWS Webstore at:

www.zgws.org

ACKNOWLEDGMENTS

Zane Grey's West Society President Terry Bolinger, Vice-President Rosanne Vrugtman, and Marketing Coordinator Ed Meyer extend their gratitude and thanks to Society members Marian Coombs, Jan Gautreaux and Tim Abner, for their assistance in making *The Zane Grey Primer* available to young people throughout the world.

Zane Grey

DEDICATION

To the next generation of Zane Grey readers

PREFACE

The *Zane Grey Primer* is a collection articles and stories written by Zane Grey (1872-1939), considered by many to be the "Father of the Western Romance Novel." He was also one of America's greatest sportsmen and adventurers. This collection was compiled by Zane Grey's West Society, a non-profit organization dedicated to educating a new generation about this great author.

This work was published for a very specific purpose: to provide teens and young adults with an introduction to Zane Grey's works. It is our hope that young readers will enjoy these stories and decide to move on to Grey's novels and outdoor adventure travelogues. In many ways, we see *The Zane Grey Primer* as our adaptation of the example set by the potato chip company that threw down the gauntlet to consumers with their challenge: "Bet You Can't Eat Just One!"

This *Primer* is not a commercial venture. Our intention is either to donate copies of this book to organizations that will pass them along to young readers, or sell them at cost to our members and others interested in Zane Grey. This allows us to achieve our goals of educating the world about Zane Grey; creating a renewed market for his works; and most importantly, introducing young readers to the marvelous adventures and word art they will find in Grey's stories.

THE ZANE GREY PRIMER

CONTENTS

Appendices

Notes
Zane Grey: Author and Adventurer
Discussion Guide for Teachers
  and Reading Group Leaders
Zane Grey Museums
List of Zane Grey Works
Invitation to Join Zane Grey's West Society

INTRODUCTION

The Zane Grey Primer is a collection of stories by a man who travelled all over the world from about 1900 to 1940. Most of his stories were about heroes and heroines of the frontier or the American West; but he also wrote great articles about fishing, hunting and outdoor adventures.

Zane Grey published his first novel in 1903, and a lot of young people have not read any of his books. That's why we've put together this "primer"—a book that introduces people to something. In this case, *The Zane Grey Primer* is intended to introduce a new generation to an author we think they will enjoy.

Each of the stories in this book is short enough to read when you have a few minutes to spare. We hope you will read one story, then another, and another. When you've read them all, maybe you will decide to try one of Zane Grey's full novels!

The Zane Grey Primer will be entertaining to adults, as well. Many of these stories were published long ago in magazines, and even Zane Grey fans haven't read them.

We hope you will enjoy reading these Zane Grey stories as much as others have over the past 100 years or so since they were first published.

Zane Grey's West Society

Zane Grey named this mountain lion "Billy."
Tales of Lonely Trails (1922)

KEN AND HAL MEET

THE MOUNTAIN LIONS

From *The Young Lion Hunter* (1911)

Ken brings his 14-year-old brother, Hal, to the North Rim of the Grand Canyon to lasso mountain lions with an old lion hunter named Hiram and two forest rangers, Dick Leslie and Jim Williams. The five of them are off on an adventure with a pack of wonderful hunting dogs. If you like this story, you may want to read Zane Grey's book for young people, The Young Lion Hunter.

We rode abreast through the forest, and I could not help seeing the pleasure in Ken's face and the wild spirit in Hal's eyes. The hounds followed Prince at an orderly trot. We struck out of the pines at half past five. Floating mists hid the lower end of the plateau, but cedar trees began to show green against the soft gray of sage. The morning had a cool touch, though there was no frost. Jogging along, we had crossed Middle Cañon and were nearing the dark line of cedar forest when Hiram, who led, held up his hand in a warning check.

"Oh, Ken! look at Prince," whispered Hal to his brother.

The hound stood stiff, head well up, nose working, and hair on his back bristling. All the other hounds whined and kept close to him.

"Prince has a scent," said Hiram. "Thar's been a cougar round hyar. I never knowed Prince to be fooled. The scent's in the wind. Hunt 'em up, Prince. Spread out thar, you dogs."

The pack commenced to work back and forth along the ridge. We neared a hollow where Prince barked eagerly. Curley answered, and likewise Queen. Mux's short, angry bow-wow showed that he was in line.

"Ringer's gone," shouted Jim. "He was farthest ahead. Shore he's struck a trail."

"Likely enough," replied Hiram. "But Ringer doesn't bay. Thar's Prince workin' over. Look sharp, youngsters, an' be ready fer some ridin'. We're close!"

The hounds went tearing through the sage, working harder and harder, calling and answering one another, all the time getting down into the hollow. Suddenly Prince began to yelp. Like a yellow dart he shot into the cedars, running head up. Curley howled his deep, full bay and led the rest of the pack up the slope in angry clamor.

"Thar off!" yelled Hiram, spurring his big horse.

"Stay with me, Kid," shouted Jim over his shoulder to Hal. The lad's pinto leaped into quick action. They were out of sight in the cedars in less than a moment. I heard Ken close behind me, and yelled to him to come along. Crashings among the cedars ahead, thud of hoofs and yells kept me going in one direction. The fiery burst of the hounds had surprised me. Such hunting was as new to me as to the boys, and from the tingling in my veins I began to feel that it was just as exciting. I remembered that Jim had said Hiram and his charger might keep the pack in sight, but the rest of us could not.

My horse was carrying me at a fast pace on the trail of someone, and he seemed to know that by keeping in this trail part of the work of breaking through the brush was already done for him. Ken's horse thundered in my rear. The sharp cedar branches struck and stung me, and I heard them hitting Ken. We climbed a ridge, found the cedars thinning out, and then there were open patches. As we faced a slope of sage I saw Hiram on his big horse.

"Ride now, boy!" I yelled to Ken.

"I'll hang to you. Cut loose!" he shouted in reply.

We hurdled the bunches of sage, and went over the brush, rocks, and gullies at breakneck speed. I heard nothing but the wind singing in my ears. Hiram's trail, plain in the yellow ground, showed me the way. Upon entering the cedars again we lost it. I stopped my horse and checked Ken. Then I called. I heard the baying of the hounds, but no answer to my signal.

"Don't say we've lost them!" cried Ken. "Come on! The hounds are close."

We burst through thickets, threaded the mazes of cedars, and galloped over sage flats till a signal cry, sharp to our right, turned us. I answered, and an exchange of signals led us into an open glade where we found Hiram, Jim, and Hal, but no sign of a hound.

"Hyar you are," said Hiram. "Now hold up, an' listen fer the hounds."

With the labored breathing of the horses filling our ears we could hear no other sound. Dismounting, I went aside a little way and turned my ear to the breeze.

"I hear Prince," I cried, instantly.

"Which way?" both men asked.

"West."

"Strange," said Hiram.

"Shore the hounds wouldn't split?" asked Jim. "Prince leave thet hot trail? Not much. But he's runnin' queer this mornin'."

"There! Now listen," I put in. "There are Prince and another hound with a deep bay."

"Thet's Curley. I hear 'em now. They're runnin' to us, an' hot. We might see a cougar any minnit. Keep a tight rein, youngsters. Mind a hoss is scared to death of a cougar."

The baying came closer and closer. Our horses threw up their ears. Hal's pinto stood up and snorted. The lad handled him well. Then at a quick cry from Jim we saw Prince cross the lower end of the flat.

There was no need to spur our mounts. The lifting of bridles served, and away we raced. Prince disappeared in a trice, then Curley, Mux, and Queen broke out of the cedars in full cry. They, too, were soon out of sight.

"Hounds runnin' wild," yelled Hiram.

The onslaught of the hunter and his charger stirred a fear in me that checked admiration. I saw the green of a low cedar-tree shake and split to let in the huge, gaunt horse with rider doubled over the saddle. Then came the crash of breaking brush and pounding of hoofs from the direction the hounds had taken. We strung out in the lane Hiram left and hung low over the pommels; and though we had his trail and followed it at only half his speed, yet the tearing and whipping we got from the cedar spikes were hard enough indeed.

A hundred rods within the forest we unexpectedly came upon Hiram, dismounted, searching the ground. Mux and Curley were with him, apparently at fault. Suddenly Mux left the little glade and, with a sullen, quick bark, disappeared under the trees. Curley sat on his haunches and yelped.

"Shore somethin's wrong," said Jim, tumbling out of his saddle. "Hiram, I see a lion track."

"Here, fellows, I see one, and it's not where you're looking," I added.

"Now what do you think I'm lookin' fer if it ain't tracks?" queried Hiram. "Hyar's one cougar track, an' thar's another. Jump off, youngsters, an' git a good look at 'em. Hyar's the trail we were on, an' thar's the other, crossin' at right angles. Both are fresh, one ain't many minnits old. Prince an' Queen hev split one way, an' Mux another. Curley, wise old hound, hung fire an' waited fer me. Whar on earth is Ringer? It ain't like him to be lost when thar's doin's like this."

"What next?" asked Jim, mounting.

"I'll put Curley on the fresher trail," replied Hiram. "An' you all ought to be able to keep within hearin' of him...Thar! Curley...Hi! Hi!"

Curley dashed off on the trail Mux had taken. Then began some hard riding. Hal and the pinto were directly in front of me, and I saw that the lad was having the ride of his life. Sometimes he ducked the cedar branches and again he was not quick enough. There were times when I thought he would be swept from his saddle, but he hung on while the pinto made a hole in the brush. More than once Hal lost his stirrup-footing. All the time that I watched him and turned to see if Ken was all right, I was getting a thrashing from the cedars. But I felt only the severest lashes. From time to time Hiram yelled. We managed to keep within earshot of Curley, and presently reached a cañon, which, judging by depth, must have been Middle Cañon.

At that point it was a barrier to our progress, but fortunately Curley did not climb the opposite slope, so we followed the rim and gained on the hound. Soon we heard Mux. Curley had caught up with him. We came to a point where the cañon was not so deep and wider, and the slopes were less rugged. Curley bayed incessantly. Mux uttered harsh howls, and both hounds in plain sight began working in a circle. Hiram reined in his horse and leaped off, while the rest of us came to a halt.

"Off now, youngsters," said Hiram, sharply. "Tie your hosses, tight. The cougar's gone up somewhat. Run along the slope an' look sharp in every cedar an' piñon, an' in every crevice of the cliffs."

Hal jumped off, but did not tie his pinto, and he was white with excitement and panting heavily. Ken left his mustang and hurried along the ledge ahead of me. Every few steps he would stop to peer cautiously around. As if he had been struck, he suddenly straightened and his voice pealed out:

"The lion! The lion! Here he is! I see him!...Oh, hurry, Hal!"

I ran toward Ken, but could not see the lion. Then I stopped to watch Mux. He ran to the edge of a low wall of stone across the cañon; he looked over, and barked fiercely. When I saw him slide down a steep slope, make for the bottom of the stone wall, and jump into the branches of a cedar I knew where to look for the lion. Then I espied a round yellow ball cunningly curled up in a mass of branches. Probably the lion had leaped into the tree from the wall.

"Treed! Treed!" I yelled. "Mux has found him."

Hiram appeared, crashing down a weathered slope.

"Hyar, everybody," he bawled. "Hustle down an' make a racket. We don't want him to jump."

Hiram and Jim rolled down and fairly cracked the stones in their descent. I shouted for the boys to come on. Hal never moved a muscle, and Ken seemed chained to the spot. Hiram turned and saw them.

"Ho, youngsters, are you scared?" shouted he.

"Yes, but I'm coming," replied Ken. Still he showed a strange vacillation. Overcome then by shame or anger, he plunged down the slope and did not halt till he was under the snarling lion.

"Back, Ken, back! You're too close," warned Hiram. "He might jump, an' if he does don't run, but drop flat. He's a Tom, a two-year-old, an' he's sassy."

"Don't care—whether he—jumps or not," panted Ken, bouncing about. "I've got to—be cured—of this—this—"

Whatever Ken had to be cured of he did not say, but I had no doubt that it was dread. I, myself, did not feel perfectly cool, by some dozens of degrees. The flaming eyes of the lion, his open mouth with its white fangs, his steady, hissing growls, the rippling of muscles as if it was his intention to leap at the hounds, were matters certainly not conducive to calmness.

"Will you—look at Mux!" shouted Ken.

The old hound had already climbed a third of the distance up to the lion.

"Hyar, Mux, you rascal coon-chaser!" yelled Hiram. "Out of thar!" He threw stones and sticks at the hound. Mux replied with his surly bark and steadily climbed on.

"I'll hev to pull him out, or that'll be a dead hound in about a minnit," said Hiram. "Watch close, Jim, an' tell me if the cougar starts down. I can't see through the thick branches. He'll git mighty nervous jest before he starts."

When Hiram mounted into the first branches of the cedar, Tom emitted an ominous growl and bunched himself into a ball, trembling all over.

"Shore he's comin'," yelled Jim.

The lion, snarling viciously, started to descend, and Hiram warily backed down. It was a ticklish moment for all of us, particularly Hiram; and as for me, what with keeping an eye on the lion and watching the boys, I had enough to do. Hal's actions were singular; he would run down the slope, then run back, wave his arms and let out an Indian yell. His brother kept dodging to and fro as if he were on hot bricks. Never before had I seen such eyes as blazed in Ken Ward's face. The lion went back up the cedar, Mux climbed laboriously on, and Hiram followed. "Fellars, mebbe he's bluffin'," said Hiram.

"Let's try him out. Now all of you grab sticks an' holler an' run at the tree as if you was goin' to kill him."

The thrashing, yelling din we made under that cedar might have alarmed even an African lion. Tom shook all over, showed his white fangs, and climbed so far up that the branches he clung to swayed alarmingly.

"Here, punch Mux out," said Jim, handing up a long pole.

The old hound hung to the tree, making it difficult to dislodge him, but at length Hiram punched him off. He fell heavily, whereupon, venting his thick battle-cry, he essayed to climb again.

"You old gladiator! Git down!" protested Hiram. "What in the tarnal dickens can we do with sich a dog? Tie him up, somebody."

Jim seized Mux and made him fast to the lasso with which Curley had already been secured.

"Wal, fellers, I can't reach him hyar. I'm goin' farther up," said the hunter.

"Rustle, now," yelled Jim.

I saw that Hiram evidently had that in mind. He climbed quickly. It was enough to make even a man catch his breath to watch him, and I heard Ken gasping. Hiram reached the middle fork of the cedar, stood erect and extended the noose of his lasso on the point of his pole. Tom, with a hiss and a snap, savagely struck at it. A second trial tempted the lion to seize the rope with his teeth. In a flash Hiram withdrew the pole and lifted a loop of the slack noose over the lion's ears. The other end of the lasso he threw down to Jim.

"Pull!" he yelled.

Jim threw all his weight into action, pulling the lion out with a crash, and giving the cedar such a tremendous shake that Hiram lost his footing. Grasping at branches and failing to hold, he fell, apparently right upon the lion. A whirling cloud of dust arose, out of which Hiram made prodigious leaps.

"Look out!" he bawled.

His actions, without words, would have been electrifying enough. As I ran to one side the lion just missed Hiram. Then with a spring that sent the stones rattling he made at Ken. The lad dove straight downhill into a thicket. When the furious lion turned on Jim, that worthy dropped the lasso and made tracks. Here the quick-witted Hiram seized the free end of the trailing lasso and tied it to a sapling. Then the wrestling lion disappeared in a thick cloud of dust.

"Dod gast the luck!" yelled Hiram, picking up Jim's lasso. "I didn't mean for you to pull him out of the tree. He'll kill himself now or git loose."

When the dust cleared away I discovered our prize stretched out at full length, frothing at the mouth. As Hiram approached, swinging the other lasso, the lion began a series of evolutions that made him resemble a wheel of yellow fur and dust. Then came a thud and he lay inert.

Hiram pounced upon him and loosened the lasso round his neck.

"I'm afraid he's done fer. But mebbe not. They're hard-lived critters. He's breathin' yet. Hyar, Leslie, help me tie his paws together...Be watchful."

As I came up the lion stirred and raised his head. Hiram ran the loop of the second lasso round the two hind paws and stretched Tom out. While in this helpless position, with no strength and scarcely any breath, he was easy to handle. With Jim and me attending strictly to orders Hiram clipped the sharp claws, tied the four paws together, took off the neck lasso and substituted a collar and chain.

"Let him breathe a little. He's comin' round all right," said Hiram. "But we're lucky. Jim, never pull another cougar clear out of a tree. Pull him off over a limb an' hang him thar while someone below ropes his hind paws. Thet's the only way, an' if we don't stick to it somebody'll git chewed up."

Ken appeared, all scratched and torn from his header into the thorny brake. As he gazed at our captive he whooped for Hal. The lad edged down the slope and approached us eagerly. He was absolutely unconscious that we were laughing at him. His face was in a flush, with brow moist and his telltale eyes protruding. Whatever the few thrilling moments had been to us, they must have been tame compared to what they had been to Hal.

"Wal, youngster, whar were you when it came off?" inquired Hiram, with a smile.

"Have we got him—really?" whispered Hal. "Shore, Kid. He's a good cougar now," answered Jim.

"Come along an' watch me put on his muzzle," said Hiram.

Hiram's method of performing this part of his work was the most hazardous of all. He thrust a stick between Tom's open jaws, and when the lion crushed it into splinters he tried another and yet another, till he found one that did not break. Then, while Tom bit on it, Hiram placed a wire loop over the animal's nose, slowly tightening it till the stick would not slip forward of the great canine teeth.

"Thar, thet's one, ready to pack to camp. We'll leave him hyar an' hunt up Prince an' Queen. They've treed the other cougar by this time."

When Jim untied Mux and Curley it was remarkable to see what little interest they had in the now helpless lion. Mux growled, then followed Curley up the slope. We all climbed out and mounted our horses.

"Hear thet!" yelled Hiram. "Thar's Prince yelpin'. Hi! Hi! Hi!"

From the cedars across the ridge rang a thrilling chorus of bays. Hiram spurred his horse and we fell in behind him at a gallop. We leveled a lane of sage in that short race, and when Hiram leaped off at the edge of the impenetrable cedar forest we were close at his heels. He disappeared and Jim and Ken followed him. I heard them smashing the dead wood, and soon a deep yell mingled with shouts and the yelps of the hounds. I waited to tie Ken's mustang, and I had to perform a like office for Hal, whose hands trembled so he could not do it. He jerked his rifle out of his scabbard.

"No, no, Hal, you won't want that. Put it back. You might shoot somebody in the excitement. Come on. Keep your wits. You can climb or dodge as well as I."

Then I dragged him into the gloomy clump of cedars whence came the uproar. First I saw Ken in a tree, climbing fast; then Mux in another, and under him the other hounds with noses skyward; and last, up in the dead topmost branches, a big tawny lion.

"Whoop!" the yell leaped past my lips. Quiet Jim was yelling; Ken was splitting the air, and Hiram let out from his cavernous chest a booming roar that almost crowned ours.

I lifted and shoved Hal into a cedar, and then turned to the grim business of the moment. Hiram's first move was to pull Mux out of the tree.

"Hyar, Leslie, grab him; he's stronger'n a hoss."

If Mux had been only a little stronger he would have broken away from me. Jim ran a rope under the collar of all the hounds; there both of us pulled them from under the lion.

"It's got to be a slip-knot," said Jim, as we fumbled with the rope. "Shore if the cougar jumps we want to be able to free the hounds quick."

Then while Hiram climbed Jim and I waited. I saw Ken in the top of a cedar on a level with the lion. Hal hugged a branch and strained his gaze, and, judging from the look of him, his heart was in his throat. Hiram's gray hat went pushing up between the dead snags, then his burly shoulders. The quivering muscles of the lion grew tense, and his lithe body crouched low. He was about to jump. His dripping jaws, his wild eyes roving for some means of escape, his tufted tail swinging against the twigs and breaking them, manifested his terror and extremity. The hunter climbed on with a rope between his teeth and a long stick in his hand.

"Git ropes ready down thar!" yelled Hiram.

My rope was new and bothersome to handle. When I got it right with a noose ready I heard a cracking of branches. Looking up, I saw the lion biting hard at a rope which circled his neck. Jim ran directly under the tree with a spread noose in his hands. Then Hiram pulled and pulled, but the lion held firmly. Whereupon Hiram threw his end of the rope down to me.

"Thar, Leslie, lend a hand."

We both pulled with might and main; still the lion was too strong. Suddenly the branch broke, letting the lion fall, kicking frantically with all four paws. Jim grasped one of the lower paws and dexterously left the noose fast on it. But only by a hair's breadth did he dodge the other whipping paw.

"Let go, Leslie," yelled Hiram.

I complied, and the rope Hiram and I had held flew up over the branches as the lion fell, and then it dropped to the ground. Hiram, plunging out of the tree, made a flying snatch for the rope, got it and held fast.

"Stretch him out, Jim," roared Hiram. "An' Leslie, stand ready to put another rope on."

The action had been fast, but it was slow to what then began. It appeared impossible for two strong men, one of them a giant, to straighten out that wrestling lion. The dust flew, the sticks snapped, the gravel pattered against the cedars. Jim went to his knees, and Hiram's huge bulk bowed under the strain. Then Jim plowed the ground flat on his stomach. I ran to his assistance and took the rope which he now held by only one hand. He got up and together we lent our efforts, getting in a strong haul on the lion. Short as that moment was it enabled Hiram to make his lasso fast to a cedar. The three of us then stretched the beast from tree to tree, after which Hiram put a third lasso on the front paws.

"A whoppin' female," said Hiram, as our captive lay helpless with swelling sides and blazing eyes. "She's nearly eight feet from tip to tip, but not extra heavy. Females never git fat. Hand me another rope."

With four lassoes in position to suit Hiram the lioness could not move. Then he proceeded to tie her paws, clip her claws, muzzle and chain her.

"I reckon you squirrels can come down now," remarked Hiram, dryly, to the brothers. "See hyar, one of these days when we git split, thar'll be mebbe no one to help me but one of you youngsters. What then?"

To Hal and Ken, who had dropped out of their perches, the old hunter's speech evidently suggested something at once frightful and enthralling.

"Shore as you're born thet's goin' to happen,' added Jim, as he wiped the sweat and dust from his face.

"I never felt—so—before in my life," said Hal, tremulously. "My whole insides went like a crazy clock when you break a spring. Then I froze—scared stiff!"

His naive confession strengthened any already favorable impression.

Ken laughed. "Kid, didn't I say it was coming to you?"

Hal did not reply to this; he had shifted his attention to the hounds. Jim was loosing them from the rope. They had ceased yelping and I was curious to know how they would regard our captive.

Prince walked within three feet of the lioness, disdaining to notice her at all, and lay down. Curley wagged his tail; Queen began to lick her sore foot; Tan wearily stretched himself for a nap; only Mux, the incorrigible, retained antipathy for our bound captive, and he growled once low and deep, and rolled his bloodshot eyes at her as if to remind her it was he who had brought her to such a pass. And, on the instant, Ringer, lame and dusty from travel, trotted into the glade, and, looking at the lioness, he gave one disgusted grunt and flopped down.

**Zane Grey helping a young woman much like Lucy
get ready to ride her mustang on a trip
to Rainbow Bridge**
Zane Grey's West Society Collection

LUCY'S RUN

Wildfire: 1910

Lucy is the daughter of a man who prides himself on having the finest race horses in the West. He isn't aware that she has befriended a young horse hunter and the wild mustang he has captured. The mustang is named Wildfire and the young man is amazed that the huge horse lets Lucy ride him. Unknown to her father, Lucy and Wildfire compete against his horse and others in a fierce horse race.

It was afternoon when all was ready for this race, and the sage was bright gray in the westering sun. Everybody was resting, waiting. The tense quiet of the riders seemed to settle upon the whole assemblage. Only the thoroughbreds were restless. They quivered and stamped and tossed their small, fine heads. They knew what was going to happen. They wanted to run. Blacks, bays, and whites were the predominating colors; and the horses and mustangs were alike in those points of race and speed and spirit that proclaimed them thoroughbreds.

Bostil himself took the covering off his favorite. Sage King was on edge. He stood out strikingly in contrast with the other horses. His sage-gray body was as sleek and shiny as satin. He had been trained to the hour. The racehorse tossed his head as he champed the bit, and every moment his muscles rippled under his fine skin. Proud, mettlesome, beautiful!

Sage King was the favorite in the betting, the Indians, who were ardent gamblers, plunging heavily on him.

Bostil saddled the horse and was long at the task.

Van stood watching. He was pale and nervous. Bostil saw this.

"Van," he said, "it's your race."

The rider reached a quick hand for bridle and horn, and when his foot touched the stirrup Sage King was in the air. He came down, springy-quick, graceful, and then he pranced into line with the other horses.

Bostil waved his hand. Then the troop of riders and racers headed for the starting-point, two miles up the valley. Macomber and Blinn were up there as the official starters of the day.

Bostil's eyes glistened. He put a friendly hand on Cordts's shoulder, an action which showed the stress of the moment. Most of the men crowded around Bostil. Sears and Hutchinson hung close to Cordts. And Holley, keeping near his employer, had keen eyes for other things than horses.

Suddenly he touched Bostil and pointed down the slope. "There's Lucy," he said. "She's ridin' out to join the bunch."

"Lucy! Where? I'd forgotten my girl! ... Where?"

"There," repeated Holly, and he pointed. Others of the group spoke up, having seen Lucy riding down.

"She's on a red hoss," said one.

"'Pears all-fired big to me—her hoss," said another. "Who's got a glass?"

Bostil had the only field-glass there and he was using it. Across the round, magnified field of vision moved a giant red horse, his mane waving like a flame. Lucy rode him. They were moving from a jumble of broken rocks a mile down the slope. She had kept her horse hidden there. Bostil felt an added stir in his pulse-beat. Certainly he had never seen a horse like this one. But the distance was long, the glass not perfect; he could not trust his sight. Suddenly that sight dimmed.

"Holley, I can't make out nothin'," he complained. "Take the glass. Give me a line on Lucy's mount."

"Boss, I don't need the glass to see that she's up on a HOSS," replied Holley, as he took the glass. He leveled it, adjusted it to his eyes, and then looked long. Bostil grew impatient. Lucy was rapidly overhauling the troop of racers on her way to the post. Nothing ever hurried or excited Holley.

"Wal, can't you see any better 'n me?" queried Bostil, eagerly.

"Come on, Holl, give us a tip before she gits to the post," spoke up a rider.

Cordts showed intense eagerness, and all the group were excited. Lucy's advent, on an unknown horse that even her father could not disparage, was the last and unexpected addition to the suspense. They all knew that if the horse was fast Lucy would be dangerous.

Holley at last spoke: "She's up on a wild stallion. He's red, like fire. He's mighty big—strong. Looks as if he didn't want to go near the bunch. Lord! what action! ... Bostil, I'd say—a great hoss!"

There was a moment's intense silence in the group round Bostil. Holley was never known to mistake a horse or to be extravagant in judgment or praise.

"A wild stallion!" echoed Bostil. "A-huh! An' she calls him Wildfire. Where'd she get him? ... Gimme thet glass."

But all Bostil could make out was a blur. His eyes were wet. He realized now that his first sight of Lucy on the strange horse had been clear and strong, and it was that which had dimmed his eyes.

"Holley, you use the glass—an' tell me what comes off," said Bostil, as he wiped his eyes with his scarf. He was relieved to find that his sight was clearing. "My God! if I couldn't see this finish!"

Then everybody watched the close, dark mass of horses and riders down the valley. And all waited for Holley to speak. "They're linin' up," began the rider. "Havin' some muss, too, it 'pears.... Bostil, thet red hoss is raisin' hell! He wants to fight. There! he's up in the air.... Boys, he's a devil—a hoss-killer like all them wild stallions.... He's plungin' at the King—strikin'! There! Lucy's got him down. She's handlin' him.... Now they've got the King on the other side. Thet's better. But Lucy's hoss won't stand. Anyway, it's a runnin' start.... Van's got the best position. Foxy Van! ... He'll be leadin' before the rest know the race's on.... Them Indian mustangs are behavin' scandalous. Guess the red stallion scared 'em. Now they're all lined up back of the post.... Ah! gun-smoke! They move.... It looks like a go."

Then Holley was silent, strained, in watching. So were all the watchers silent. Bostil saw far down the valley a moving, dark line of horses.

"THEY'RE OFF! THEY'RE OFF!" called Holley, thrillingly.

Bostil uttered a deep and booming yell, which rose above the shouts of the men round him and was heard even in the din of Indian cries. Then as quickly as the yells had risen they ceased.

Holley stood up on the rock with leveled glass.

"Mac's dropped the flag. It's a sure go. Now! ... Van's out there front—inside. The King's got his stride. Boss, the King's stretchin' out! ... Look! Look! see thet red hoss leap! ... Bostil, he's runnin' down the King! I knowed it. He's like lightnin'. He's pushin' the King over—off the course! See him plunge! Lord! Lucy can't pull him! She goes up—down—tossed—but she sticks like a burr. Good, Lucy! Hang on! ... My Gawd, Bostil, the King's thrown! He's down! ... He comes up, off the course. The others flash by.... Van's out of the race! An', Bostil—an', gentlemen, there ain't anythin' more to this race but a red hoss!"

Bostil's heart gave a great leap and then seemed to stand still. He was half cold, half hot.

What a horrible, sickening disappointment. Bostil rolled out a cursing query. Holley's answer was short and sharp. The King was out! Bostil raved. He could not see. He could not believe. After all the weeks of preparation, of excitement, of suspense—only this! There was no race. The King was out! The thing did not seem possible. A thousand thoughts flitted through Bostil's mind. Rage, impotent rage, possessed him. He cursed Van, he swore he would kill that red stallion. And someone shook him hard. Someone's incisive words cut into his thick, throbbing ears: "Luck of the game! The King ain't beat! He's only out!"

Then the rider's habit of mind asserted itself and Bostil began to recover. For the King to fall was hard luck. But he had not lost the race! Anguish and pride battled for mastery over him. Even if the King were out it was a Bostil who would win the great race.

"He ain't beat!" muttered Bostil. "It ain't fair! He's run off the track by a wild stallion!"

His dimmed sight grew clear and sharp. And with a gasp he saw the moving, dark line take shape as horses. A bright horse was in the lead. Brighter and larger he grew. Swiftly and more swiftly he came on. The bright color changed to red. Bostil heard Holley calling and Cordts calling—and other voices, but he did not distinguish what was said. The line of horses began to bob, to bunch. The race looked close, despite what Holley had said. The Indians were beginning to lean forward, here and there uttering a short, sharp yell. Everything within Bostil grew together in one great, throbbing, tingling mass. His rider's eye, keen once more, caught a gleam of gold above the red, and that gold was Lucy's hair. Bostil forgot the King.

Then Holley bawled into his ear, "They're half-way!"

The race was beautiful. Bostil strained his eyes. He gloried in what he saw—Lucy low over the neck of that red stallion. He could see plainer now. They were coming closer. How swiftly! What a splendid race! But it was too swift—it would not last. The Indians began to yell, drowning the hoarse shouts of the riders. Out of the tail of his eye Bostil saw Cordts and Sears and Hutchinson. They were acting like crazy men. Strange that horse-thieves should care! The million thrills within Bostil coalesced into one great shudder of rapture. He grew wet with sweat. His stentorian voice took up the call for Lucy to win.

"Three-quarters!" bowled Holley into Bostil's ear. "An' Lucy's give thet wild hoss free rein! Look, Bostil! You never in your life seen a hoss run like thet!"

Bostil never had. His heart swelled. Something shook him. Was that his girl—that tight little gray burr half hidden in the huge stallion's flaming mane? The distance had been close between Lucy and the bunched riders.

But it lengthened. How it widened! That flame of a horse was running away from the others. And now they were close—coming into the home stretch. A deafening roar from the onlookers engulfed all other sounds. A straining, stamping, arm-flinging horde surrounded Bostil.

Bostil saw Lucy's golden hair whipping out from the flame-streaked mane. And then he could only see that red brute of a horse. Wildfire before the wind! Bostil thought of the leaping prairie flame, storm-driven.

On came the red stallion—on—on! What a tremendous stride! What a marvelous recovery! What ease! What savage action!

He flashed past, low, pointed, long, going faster every magnificent stride—winner by a dozen lengths.

"Lightning" by Stanley Adams
The Outing Magazine (April 1910)

LIGHTNING

The Outing Magazine, (April 1910)

Lightning is a wild mustang who doesn't want to be captured. Lee and Cuth Stewart are brothers who love the magnificent horse and chase him across some of the West's most remote country. If you like this story, you may want to read one of Zane Grey's novels about mustangs like Wildfire, Wild Horse Mesa *or* Valley of Wild Horses.

REWARD: $500 WILL BE PAID FOR THE DEATH OF LIGHTNING, LEADER OF THE SEVIER RANGE OF WILD HORSES. UTAH CATTLE COMPANY.

This notice, with a letter coming by stage and messenger to the Stewarts, brightened what had been a dull prospect. Seldom did a whole year's work, capturing and corralling mustangs in the canyons and on the plateaus, pay them half as much as the reward offered for this one stallion. The last season had been a failure altogether. A string of pintos and mustangs, representing months of hazardous toil, had climbed out of a canyon corral and escaped to their old haunts. So on the strength of this opportunity the brothers packed and rode out of Fredonia across the Arizona line into Utah.

Two days took them beyond and above the Pink Cliffs to the White Sage plateau, and there the country became new to them. From time to time a solitary sheepherder, encountered with his flocks on a sage slope, set them in the right direction, and on the seventh day they reached Bain, the most southerly of the outposts of the big Utah ranches. It consisted of a water hole, a corral, a log cabin, and some range riders.

Lee and Cuth Stewart were tall, lean Mormons, as bronzed as desert Navajos, cool, silent, gray-eyed, still-faced. Both wore crude homespun garments much the worse for wear; boots that long before had given the best in them; laced leather wristbands thin and shiny from contact with lassoes; and old gray slouch hats that would have disgraced cowboys.

But this threadbare effect did not apply to the rest of the outfit, which showed a care that must have been in proportion to its hard use. And the five beautiful mustangs, Bess in particular, proved that the Stewarts were Indians at the end of every day, for they certainly had camped where there were grass and water. The pack of hounds shared interest with the mustangs, and the leader, a great yellow, somber-eyed hound, Dash by name, could have made friends with everybody had he felt inclined.

"We calculated, boys," held forth the foreman, "that if anybody could round up Lightnin' an' his bunch it'd be you. Every ranger between here an' Marysvale has tried an' failed. Lightnin' is a rare cute stallion. He has more than hoss sense. For two years now no one has been in rifle shot of him, for the word has long since gone out to kill him.

"It's funny to think how many rangers have tried to corral him, trap him, or run him down. He's been a heap of trouble to all the ranchers. He goes right into a bunch of hosses, fights an' kills the stallions, an' leads off what he wants of the rest. His band is scattered all over, an' no man can count 'em, but he's got at least five hundred hosses off the ranges. An' he's got to be killed or there won't be a safe grazin' spot left in Sevier County."

"How're we to know this hoss's trail when we do cross it?" asked Lee Stewart.

"You can't miss it. His right foretrack has a notch that bites in clean every step he takes. One of my rangers came in yesterday an' reported fresh sign of Lightnin' at Cedar Springs, sixteen miles north along the red ridge there. An' he's goin' straight for his hidin' place. Whenever he's been hard chased he hits it back up there an' lays low for a while. It's rough country, though I reckon it won't be to you canyon fellers."

"How about water?"

"Good chances for water beyond Cedar, I reckon, though I don't know any springs. It's rare an' seldom any of us ever work up as far as Cedar. A scaly country up that way—black sage, an' that's all."

The Stewarts reached Cedar Springs that afternoon. It was a hot place; a few cedars, struggling for existence, lifted dead twisted branches to the sun; a scant growth of grass greened the few shady spots, and a thin stream of water ran between glistening borders of alkali. A drove of mustangs had visited the spring since dawn and had obliterated all tracks made before.

While Cuth made camp Lee rode up the ridge to get a look at the country. "We're just on the edge of wild-hoss country," he said to Cuth when he returned. "That stallion probably had a picked bunch an' was drivin' them higher up. It's gettin' hot these days and the browse is witherin'. I see old deer sign on the ridge, an' cougar, an' coyote sign trailin' after. They're all makin' fer higher up. I reckon we'll find 'em all on Sevier plateau."

"Did you see the plateau?" asked Cuth.

"Plain. Near a hundred miles away yet. Just a long flat ridge black with timber. Then there's the two snow peaks, Terrill an' Hilgard, pokin' up their cold noses. I reckon the plateau rises off these ridges, an' the Sevier River an' the mountains are on the other side. So we'll push on for the plateau. We might come up with Lightnin' and his bunch."

Sunset found them halting at a little water hole among a patch of cedars and boulders.

Cuth slipped the packs and Lee measured out the oats for the mustangs. Then the brothers set about getting supper for themselves.

Cuth had the flour and water mixed to a nicety and Lee had the Dutch oven on some red-hot coals when, moved by a common instinct, they stopped work and looked up.

The five mustangs were not munching their oats; their heads were up. Bess the keenest of the quintet, moved restlessly and then took a few steps toward the opening in the cedars.

"Bess!" called Lee, sternly. The mare stopped.

"She's got a scent," whispered Cuth, reaching for his rifle. "Mebbe it's a cougar."

"Mebbe, but I never knowed Bess to go lookin' up one... Hist! Look at Dash."

The yellow hound had risen from among his pack and stood warily shifting his nose. He sniffed the wind, turned round and round, and slowly stiffened with his head pointing up the ridge. The other hounds caught something, at least the manner of their leader, and became restless.

"Down, Dash, down," said Lee, and then with a smile to Cuth, "Did you hear it?"

"Hear what?"

"Listen!"

The warm breeze came down in puffs from the ridge: it rustled the cedars and blew fragrant whiffs of smoke into the hunters' faces, and presently it bore a call, a low, prolonged call.

Cuth rose noiselessly to his feet and stood still. So horses, hounds, and men waited listening. The sound broke the silence again, much clearer, a keen, sharp whistle. The third time it rang down from the summit of the ridge, splitting the air, strong, trenchant, the shrill, fiery call of a challenging stallion.

Bess reared an instant straight up and came down quivering.

"Look!" whispered Lee, tensely.

On the summit of the bare ridge stood a noble horse clearly silhouetted against the purple and gold of sunset sky. He was an iron-gray, and he stood wild and proud, with long silver-white mane waving in the wind.

"Lightnin'!" exclaimed Cuth.

He stood there one moment, long enough to make a picture for the wild horse hunters that would never be forgotten; then he moved back along the ridge and disappeared. Other horses, blacks and bays, showed above the sage for a moment, and they, too passed out of sight.

Before daylight the brothers were up and at dawn filed out of the cedar grove. The trained horses scarcely rattled a stone, and the hounds trotted ahead mindful of foxes and rabbits brushed out of the sage as they held back their chase.

The morning passed and the afternoon waned. Green willows began to skirt the banks of a sandy wash and the mustangs sniffed as if they smelled water. Presently the Stewarts entered a rocky corner refreshingly bright and green with grass, trees, and flowers and pleasant with the murmur of bees and fall of water.

A heavily flowing spring gushed from under a cliff, dashed down over stones to form a pool, and ran out to seep away and lose itself in the sandy wash. Flocks of blackbirds chattered around the pool and rabbits darted everywhere.

"It'd take a hull lot of chasin' to drive a mustang from comin' regular to that spring," commented Cuth.

"Sure, it's a likely place, an' we can make a corral here in short order."

In a day's hard work, they completed the corral. The pool was enclosed, except on the upper side where the water tumbled over a jumble of rocks, a place no horse could climb out, and on the lower side where they left the opening for the ponderous pine-log gate which would trap the mustangs once they had entered the corral.

At nightfall they were ready and waiting for their quarry. At midnight the breeze failed and a dead stillness set in. It was not broken until the afterpart of the night and then, suddenly, by the shrill, piercing neigh of a mustang. The Stewarts raised themselves sharply and looked at each other thoughtfully in the dark.

"Did you hear thet?" asked Lee.

"I just did. Sounded like Bess."

"It was Bess, darn her black hide. She never did that before."

"Mebbe she's winded Lightnin'."

"Mebbe. But she ain't hobbled, an' if she'd whistle like thet for him she's liable to make off after him. Now, what to do?"

"It's too late. I warned you before. We can't spoil what may be a chance to get the stallion. Let Bess alone. Many's the time she's had a chance to make off an' didn't do it. Let's wait."

"Reckon it's all we can do now. If she called thet stallion, it proves one thing—we can't never break a wild mare perfectly. The wild spirit may sleep in her blood, mebbe for years, but some time it'll answer to —"

"Shut up—listen!" interrupted Cuth.

From far up on the ridge came down the faint rattling of stones.

"Mustangs—an' they're comin' down," said Lee.

"I see 'em!" whispered Cuth.

It was an anxious moment, for the mustangs had to pass hunters and hounds before entering the gate. A black bobbing line wound out of the cedars. Then the starlight showed the line to be the mustangs marching in single file. They passed with drooping heads, hurrying a little toward the last and unsuspiciously entered the corral gate.

"Twenty-odd," whispered Lee, "but all blacks an' bays. The leader wasn't in that bunch. Mebbe it wasn't his—"

Among the cedars rose the peculiar halting thump of hobbled horses trying to cover ground, and following that snorts and crashings of brush and the pound of plunging hoofs. Then out of the cedars moved two shadows, the first a great gray horse with snowy mane, the second a small, graceful, shiny black mustang.

Lightning and Bess!

The stallion, in the fulfillment of a conquest such as had made him famous on the wild ranges, was magnificent in action and mien. Wheeling about her, whinnying, cavorting, he arched his splendid neck and pushed his head against her. His importunity was that of a master.

Suddenly Bess snorted and whirled down the trail. Lightning whistled one short blast of anger or terror and thundered after the black. Bess was true to her desert blood at the last. They vanished in the gray shadow of the cedars, as a stream of frightened mustangs poured out of the corral in a clattering roar.

Gradually the dust settled. Cuth looked at Lee and Lee looked at Cuth. For a while neither spoke. Cuth generously forbore saying: "I told you so." The failure of their plan was only an incident of horse wrangling and in no wise discomfited them. But Lee was angry at his favorite.

"You was right, Cuth," he said. "That mare played us at the finish. Ketched when she was a yearling, broke the best of any mustang we ever had, trained with us for five years, an' helped down many a stallion—an' she runs off wild with that big, white-maned brute!"

"Well, they make a team an' they'll stick," replied Cuth. "An' so'll we stick, if we have to chase them to the Great Salt Basin."

Next morning when the sun tipped the ridge rosy red, Lee put the big yellow hound on the notched track of the stallion, and the long trail began. At noon the hunters saw him heading his blacks across a rising plain, the first step of the mighty plateau stretching to the northward.

As they climbed, grass and water became more frequent along the trail. For the most part Lee kept on the tracks of the mustang leader without the aid of the hound; Dash was used in the grass and on the scaly ridges where the trail was hard to find.

The succeeding morning Cuth spied Lightning watching them from a high point. Another day found them on top of the plateau, among the huge brown pine trees and patches of snow and clumps of aspen. It took two days to cross the plateau—sixty miles. Lightning did not go down, but doubled on his trail. Rimming a plateau was familiar work for the hunters, and twice they came within sight of the leader and his band.

Sometimes for hours the hunters had him in sight, and always beside him was the little black they knew to be Bess. There was no mistaking her.

There came a day when Lightning cut out all of his band except Bess, and they went on alone. They made a spurt and lost the trailers from sight for two days. Then Bess dropped a shoe and the pursuers came up.

As she grew lamer and lamer, the stallion showed his mettle. He did not quit her, but seemed to grow more cunning as pursuit closed in on them, choosing the open places where he could see far and browsing along, covering rods where formerly he had covered miles.

One day the trail disappeared on stony ground, and there Dash came in for his share. Behind them the Stewarts climbed a very high round-topped mesa, buttressed and rimmed by cracked cliffs.

It was almost insurmountable. They reached the summit by a narrow watercourse to find a wild and lonesome level rimmed by crags and gray walls. There were cedars and fine thin grass growing on the plateau.

"Corralled!" said Lee, laconically, as his keen eye swept the surroundings. "He's never been here before an' there's no way off this mesa except by the back trail, which we'll close."

After fencing the split in the wall the brothers separated and rode around the rim of the mesa. Lightning had reached the end of his trail; he was caught in a trap.

Lee saw him flying like a gleam through the cedars, and suddenly came upon Bess limping painfully along. He galloped up, roped her, and led her, a tired and crippled mustang, back to the place selected for camp.

"Played out eh?" said Cuth, as he smoothed the dusty neck. "Well, Bess, you can rest up an' help us ketch the stallion. There's good grazin' here, an' we can go down for water."

For their operations the hunters chose the highest part of the mesa, a level cedar forest. Opposite a rampart of the cliff wall they cut a curved line of cedars, dropping them close together to form a dense, impassable fence. This enclosed a good space free from trees. From the narrowest point, some twenty yards wide, they cut another line of cedars running diagonally back a mile into the center of the mesa. What with this labor and going down every day to take the mustangs to water, nearly a week elapsed.

"It'd be somethin' to find out how long thet stallion could go without waterin'," said Lee. "But we'll make his tongue hang out tomorrow! An' just for spite we'll break him with Black Bess."

Daylight came cool and misty; the veils unrolled in the valleys, the purple curtains of the mountains lifted to the snow peaks and became clouds; and then the red sun burned out of the east.

"If he runs this way," said Lee, as he mounted Black Bess, "drive him back. Don't let him in the corral till he's plumb tired and worn out."

The mesa sloped slightly eastward and the cedar forest soon gave place to sage and juniper. At the extreme eastern point of the mesa Lee jumped Lightning out of a clump of bushes. A race ensued for half the length of the sage flat, then the stallion made into the cedars and disappeared.

Lee slowed down, trotting up the easy slope, and cut across somewhat to the right. Not long afterwards he heard Cuth yelling and saw Lightning tearing through the scrub. Lee went on to the point where he had left Cuth and waited.

Soon the pound of hoofs thudded through the forest, coming nearer and nearer. Lightning appeared straight ahead, running easily. At sight of Lee and the black mare he snorted viciously and, veering to the left, took to the open.

Lee watched him with sheer admiration. He had a beautiful stride and ran seemingly without effort. Then Cuth galloped up and reined in a spent and foam-flecked mustang.

"That stallion can run some," was his tribute.

"He sure can. Change hosses now an' be ready to fall in line when I chase him back."

With that Lee coursed away and soon crossed the trail of Lightning and followed it at a sharp trot, threading in and out of the aisles and glades of the forest. He passed through to the rim and circled half the mesa before he saw the stallion again. Lightning stood on a ridge looking backward. When the hunter yelled, the stallion leaped as if he had been shot and plunged down the ridge.

Lee headed to cut him off from the cedars, but he forged to the front, gained the cedar level, and twinkled in and out of the clump of trees. Again Lee slowed down to save his mustang.

Bess was warming up and Lee wanted to see what she could do at close range. Keeping within sight of Lightning the hunter chased him leisurely round and round the forest, up and down the sage slopes, along the walls, at last to get him headed for the only open stretch on the mesa. Lee rode across a hollow and came out on the level only a few rods behind him.

"Hi! Hi! Hi!" yelled the hunter, spurring Bess forward like a black streak.

Uttering a piercing snort of terror the gray stallion lunged out, for the first time panic-stricken, and lengthened his stride in a way that was wonderful to see. Then at the right moment Cuth darted from his hiding place, whooping at the top of his voice and whirling his lasso. Lightning won that race down the open stretch, but it cost him his best.

At the turn he showed his fear and plunged wildly first to the left then to the right. Cuth pushed him relentlessly, while Lee went back, tied up Bess, and saddled Billy, a wiry mustang of great endurance.

Then the two hunters remorselessly hemmed Lightning between them, turned him where they wished, at last to run him around the corner of the fence of cut cedars down the line through the narrow gate into the corral prepared for him.

"Hold hard," said Lee to Cuth. "I'll go in an' drive him round an' round till he's done; then when I yell you stand to one side an' rope him as he goes out."

Lightning ran around the triangular space, plunged up the steep walls, and crashed over the dead cedars. Then as sense and courage gave way more and more to terror he broke into desperate headlong flight. He ran blindly, and every time he passed the guarded gateway, his eyes were wilder and his stride more labored.

"Hi! Hi! Hi!" yelled Lee.

Cuth pulled out of the opening and hid behind the line of cedars, his lasso swinging loosely. Lightning saw the vacated opening and sprang forward with a hint of his old speed. As he passed through, a yellow loop flashed in the sun, circling, shimmering, and he seemed to run right into it. The loop whipped close around the glossy neck and the rope stretched taut. Cuth's mustang staggered under the violent shock, went to his knees, but struggled up and held. Lightning reared aloft.

Then Lee, darting up in a cloud of dust, shot his lasso. The noose nipped the right foreleg of the stallion. He plunged and for an instant there was a wild straining struggle, then he fell heaving and groaning. In a twinkling Lee sprang off and, slipping the rope that threatened to strangle Lightning replaced it by a stout halter and made this fast to a cedar.

Whereupon the Stewarts stood back and gazed at their prize. Lightning was badly spent, but not to a dangerous extent, dabbled with foam but no fleck of blood appeared; his superb coat showed scratches, but none cut the flesh. He was up after a while, panting heavily and trembling in all his muscles. He was a beaten horse, but he showed no viciousness, only the wild fear of a trapped animal. He eyed Bess, then the hunters, and last the halter.

"Lee, will you look at him! Will you just look at thet mane!" ejaculated Cuth.

"Well," replied Lee, "I reckon that reward, an' then some, can't buy him."

Monty Price faced a wildfire much like this one in Montana
"Elk Bath", John McColgan, Bureau of Land Management,
Alaska Fire Service. Alaskan Type I Incident Management Team

MONTY PRICE'S NIGHTINGALE

The Popular Magazine (May 7, 1915)

Monty Price was a cowboy who didn't hold a job for very long until a range fire and a little girl gave him a chance to show his worth. If you enjoy this story, you may want to buy The Wolf Tracker and Other Stories.

Around camp fires they cursed him in hearty cowboy fashion, and laid upon him the bane of their ill will. They said that Monty Price had no friend—that no foreman or rancher ever trusted him—that he never spent a dollar—that he would not keep a job—that there must be something crooked about a fellow who bunked and worked alone, who quit every few months to ride away, no one knew where, and who returned to the ranges, haggard and thin and shaky, hunting for another place.

He had been drunk somewhere, and the wonder of it was that no one in the Tonto Forest Ranges had ever seen him drink a drop. Red Lake and Gallatin and Bellville knew him, but no more of him than the ranges. He went farther afield, they said, and hinted darker things than a fling at faro or a fondness for red liquor.

But there was no rancher, no cowboy from one end of the vast range country to another who did not admit Monty Price's preeminence in those peculiar attributes of his calling. He was a magnificent rider; he had an iron and cruel hand with a horse, yet he never killed or crippled his mount; he possessed the Indian's instinct for direction; he never failed on the trail of lost stock; he could ride an outlaw and brand a wild steer and shoe a vicious mustang as bragging cowboys swore they could; and supreme test of all he would endure, without complaint, long toilsome hours in the piercing wind and freezing sleet and blistering sun.

"I'll tell you what," said old Abe Somers, "I've ranched from the Little Big Horn to the Pecos, an' I've seen a sight of cow-punchers in my day. But Monty Price's got 'em all skinned. It shore is too bad he's unreliable—packin' off the way he does, jest when he's the boy most needed. Some mystery about Monty."

The extra duty, the hard task, the problem with stock or tools or harness—these always fell to Monty. His most famous trick was to offer to take a comrade's night shift.

So it often happened that while the cowboys lolled round their camp fire, Monty Price, after a hard day's riding, would stand out the night guard, in rain and snow. But he always made a bargain. He sold his service. And the boys were wont to say that he put his services high.

Still they would never have grumbled at that if Monty had ever spent a dollar. He saved his money. He never bought any fancy boots or spurs or bridles or scarfs or chaps; and his cheap jeans and saddles were the jest of his companions.

Nevertheless, in spite of Monty's shortcomings, he rode in the Tonto on and off for five years before he made an enemy.

There was a cowboy named Bart Muncie who had risen to be a foreman, and who eventually went to ranching on a small scale. He acquired a range up in the forest country where grassy valleys and parks lay between the wooded hills, and here in a wild spot among the pines he built a cabin for his wife and baby.

It came about that Monty went to work for Muncie, and rode for him for six months. Then, in a dry season, with Muncie short of help and with long drives to make, Monty quit in his inexplicable way and left the rancher in dire need. Muncie lost a good deal of stock that fall, and he always blamed Monty for it.

Some weeks later it chanced that Muncie was in Bellville the very day Monty returned from his latest mysterious absence. And the two met in a crowded store.

Monty appeared vastly different from the lean-jawed, keen-eyed, hard-riding cowboy of a month back. He was haggard and thin and shaky and spiritless and somber.

"See here, Monty Price," said Muncie, with stinging scorn, "I reckon you'll spare me a minute of your precious time."

"I reckon so," replied Monty.

Muncie used up more than the allotted minute in calling Monty every bad name known to the range.

"An' the worst of all you are is that you're a liar!" concluded the rancher passionately. "I relied on you an' you failed me. You lost me a herd of stock. Put me back a year! An' for what? God only knows what! We ain't got you figgered here—not that way. But after this trick you turned me, we all know you're not square. An' I go on record callin' you as you deserve. You're no good. You've got a streak of yellow, an' you sneak off now an' then to indulge it. An' most of all you're a liar! Now, if it ain't all so—flash your gun!"

But Monty Price did not draw.

The scorn and abuse of the cowboys might never have been, for all the effect it had on Monty. He did not see it or feel it. He found employment with a rancher named Wentworth, and went at his work in the old, inimitable manner, that was at once the admiration and despair of his fellows. He rolled out of his blankets in the gray dawn, and he was the last to roll in at night.

In a week all traces of his weakened condition had vanished, and he grew strong and dark and hard, once more like iron. And then again he was up to his old tricks, more intense than ever, eager and gruff at bargaining his time, obsessed by the one idea—to make money.

To Monty the long, hot, dusty, blasting days of summer were as moments. Time flew for him. The odd jobs; the rough trails; the rides without water or food; the long stands in the cold rain; the electric storms when the lightning played around and cracked in his horse's mane, and the uneasy herd bawled and milled—all these things that were the everlasting torment of his comrades were as nothing to Monty Price.

And when the first pay day came and Monty tucked away a little roll of greenbacks inside his vest, and kept adding to it as one by one his comrades paid him for some bargained service—then in Monty Price's heart began the low and insistent and sweetly alluring call of the thing that had ruined him. Thereafter sleeping or waking, he lived in a dream, with that music in his heart, and the hours were fleeting.

On the mountain trails, in the noonday heat of the dusty ranges, in the dark, sultry nights with their thunderous atmosphere he was always listening to that song of his nightingale. To his comrades he seemed a silent, morose, greedy cowboy, a demon for work, with no desire for friendship, no thought of home or kin, no love of a woman or a horse or anything, except money. To Monty himself, his whole inner life grew rosier and mellower and richer as day by day his nightingale sang sweeter and louder.

And that song was a song of secret revel—far away—where he gave up to this wind of flame that burned within him—where a passionate and irresistible strain in his blood found its outlet—where wanton red lips whispered, and wanton eyes, wine dark and seductive, lured him, and wanton arms twined around him.

The rains failed to come that summer. The gramma grass bleached on the open ranges and turned yellow up in the parks. But there was plenty of grass and water to last out the fall. It was fire the ranchers feared. And it came.

One morning above the low, gray-stoned and black-fringed mountain range rose clouds of thick, creamy smoke. There was fire on the other side of the mountain. But unless the wind changed and drew fire in over the pass there was no danger on that score. The wind was right; it seldom changed at that season, though sometimes it blew a gale. Still the ranchers grew more anxious. The smoke clouds rolled up and spread and hid the top of the mountain, and then lifted slow, majestic columns of white and yellow toward the sky.

On the day that Wentworth, along with other alarmed ranchers, sent men up to fight the fire in the pass, Monty Price quit his job and rode away. He did not tell anybody. He just took his little pack and his horse, and in the confusion of the hour he rode away. For days he felt that his call might come at any moment, and finally it had come. It did not occur to him that he was quitting Wentworth at a most critical time. It would not have made any difference to him if it had occurred to him.

He rode away with bells in his heart. He felt like a boy at the prospect of a wonderful adventure. He felt like a man who had toiled and slaved, whose ambition had been supreme, and who had reached the pinnacle where his longing would be gratified.

His road led to the right away from the higher ground and the timber. To his left the other road wound down the ridge to the valley below and stretched on through straggling pines and clumps of cedar toward the slopes and the forests. Monty had ridden that road a thousand times. For it led to Muncie's range. And as Monty's keen eye swept on over the parks and the thin wedges of pine to the black mass to timber beyond he saw something that made him draw up with a start.

Clearly defined against the blue-black swelling slope was a white and and yellow cloud of smoke. It was moving. At thirty miles distance, that it could be seen to move at all was proof of the great speed with which it was traveling.

"She's caught!" he ejaculated. "Way down on this side. An' she'll burn over. Nothin' can save the range!"

He watched, and those keen, practiced eyes made out the changing, swelling columns of smoke, the widening path, the creeping dim red.

"Reckon that'll surprise Wentworth's outfit," soliloquized Monty thoughtfully. "It doesn't surprise me none. An' Muncie, too. His cabin's up there in the valley."

It struck Monty suddenly that the wind blew hard in his face. It was sweeping straight down the valley toward him. It was bringing that fire. Swift on the wind!

"One of them sudden changes of wind!" he said. "Veered right around! An' Muncie's range will go. An' his cabin!"

Straightway Monty grew darkly thoughtful. He had remembered seeing Muncie with Wentworth's men on the way to the pass. In fact, Muncie was the leader of this fire-fighting brigade.

"Sure he's fetched down his wife an' the baby," he muttered. "I didn't see them. But sure he must have."

Monty's sharp gaze sought the road for tracks. No fresh track showed! Muncie must have taken his family over the short-cut trail. Certainly he must have! Monty remembered Muncie's wife and child. The woman had hated him. But little Del with her dancing golden curls and her blue eyes—she had always had a ready smile for him.

It came to Monty then suddenly, strangely, that little Del would have loved him if he had let her. Where was she now? Safe at Wentworth's, without a doubt. But then she might not be. Muncie had certainly no fears of fire in the direction of home, not with the wind in the north and no prospect of change. It was quite possible— it was probable that the rancher had left his family at home that morning.

Monty experienced a singular shock. It had occurred to him to ride down to Muncie's cabin and see if the woman and child had been left. And whether or not he found them there the matter of getting back was a long chance. That wind was strong—that fire was sweeping down. How murky, red, sinister the slow-moving cloud!

"I ain't got a lot of time to decide," he said. His face turned pale and beads of sweat came out upon his brow.

That sweet little golden-haired Del, with her blue eyes and her wistful smile! Monty saw her as if she had been there. Then like lightning flashed back the thought that he was on his way to his revel. And the fires of hell burst in his veins. And more deadly sweet than any siren music rang the song of his nightingale in his heart. Neither honor nor manliness had ever stood between him and his fatal passion.

He was in a swift, golden dream, with the thick fragrance of wine, and the dark, mocking, luring eyes on him. All this that was more than life to him —to give it up—to risk it—to put if off an hour! He felt the wrenching pang of something deep hidden in his soul, beating its way up, torturing him. But it was strange and mighty.

In that terrible moment it decided for him; and the smile of a child was stronger than the unquenchable and blasting fire of his heart.

Monty untied his saddle pack and threw it aside; and then with tight-shut jaw he rode down the steep descent to the level valley. His horse was big and strong and fast. He was fresh, too, and in superb condition.

Once down on the hard-packed road he broke into a run, and it took an iron arm to hold him from extending himself. Monty calculated on saving the horse for the run back. He had no doubt that would be a race with fire. And he had been in forest fires more than once...

Muncie's cabin was a structure of logs and clapboards, standing in a little clearing, with the great pines towering all around. Monty saw the child, little Del, playing in the yard with a dog. He called. The child heard, and being frightened ran into the cabin. The dog came barking toward Monty. He was a big, savage animal, a trained watchdog. But he recognized Monty.

Hurrying forward, Monty went to the open door and called Mrs. Muncie. There was no response. He called again. And while he stood there waiting, listening, above the roar of the wind he heard a low, dull, thundering sound, like a waterfall in a flooded river. It sent the blood rushing back to his heart, leaving him cold. He had not a single instant to lose.

"Mrs. Muncie," he called louder. "Come out! Bring the child! It's Monty Price. There's forest fire! Hurry!"

He stepped into the cabin. There was no one in the big room—or the kitchen. He grew hurried now. The child was hiding. Finally he found her in the clothespress, and he pulled her out. She was frightened. She did not recognize him.

"Del, is your mother home?" he asked.

The child shook her head.

With that Monty picked her up, along with a heavy shawl he saw, and, hurrying out, he ran down to the corral. Muncie's horses were badly frightened now. Monty set little Del down, threw the shawl into a watering trough, and then he let down the bars of the gate.

The horses pounded out in a cloud of dust. Monty's horse was frightened, too, and almost broke away. There was now a growing roar on the wind. It seemed right upon him. Yet he could not see any fire or smoke. The dog came to him, whining and sniffing.

With swift hands Monty soaked the shawl thoroughly in the water, and then wrapping it round little Del and holding her tight, he mounted. The horse plunged and broke and plunged again—then leaped out straight and fast down the road. And Monty's ears seemed pierced and filled by a terrible, thundering roar.

He had to race with fire. He had to beat the wind of flame to the open parks. Ten miles of dry forest, like powder! Though he had never seen it, he knew fire backed by heavy wind could rage through dry pine faster than a horse could run.

Yet something in Monty Price welcomed this race. He goaded the horse. Then he looked back.

Through the aisles of the forest he saw a strange, streaky, murky something, moving, alive, shifting up and down, never an instant the same. It must have been the wind, the heat before the fire. He seemed to see through it, but there was nothing beyond, only opaque, dim, mustering clouds.

Ahead of him, down the road, low under the spreading trees, floated swiftly some kind of a medium, like a transparent veil. It was neither smoke nor air. It carried pin points of light, sparks, that resembled atoms of dust floating in sunlight. It was a wave of heat propelled before the storm of fire. Monty did not feel pain, but he seemed to be drying up, parching. All was so strange and unreal—the swift flight between the pines, now growing ghostly in the dimming light—the sense of rushing, overpowering force—and yet absolute silence. But that light burden against his breast—the child—was not unreal.

He must have been insane, he thought, not to be overcome in spirit. But he was not. He felt loss of something, some kind of sensation he ought to have had. But he rode that race keener and better than any race he had ever before ridden. He had but to keep his saddle—to dodge the snags of the trees—to guide the maddened horse. No horse ever in the world had run so magnificent a race.

He was outracing wind and fire. But he was running in terror. For miles he held that long, swift, tremendous stride without a break. He was running to his death whether he distanced the fire or not. For nothing could stop him now except a bursting heart. Already he was blind, Monty thought.

And then, it appeared to Monty, although his steed kept fleeting on faster and faster, that the wind of flame was gaining. The air was too thick to breathe. It seemed ponderous—not from above, but from behind. It had irresistible weight. It pushed Monty and his horse onward in their flight—straws on the crest of a cyclone.

Ahead there was light through the forest. He made out a white, open space of grass. A park! And the horse, like a demon, hurtled onward, with his smoothness of action gone, beginning to break.

A wave of wind, blasting in its heat, like a blanket of fire, rolled over Monty. He saw the lashing tongues of flame above him in the pines. The storm had caught him. It forged ahead. He was riding under a canopy of fire. Burning pine cones, like torches, dropped all around him, upon him.

A terrible blank sense of weight, of agony, of suffocation—of the air turning to fire! He was drooping, withering when he flashed from the pines out into an open park. The horse broke and plunged and went down, reeking, white, in convulsions, killed on his feet. There was fire in his mane. Monty fell with him, and lay in the grass, the child in his arms.

Fire in the grass—fire at his legs roused him. He got up. The park was burning over. It was enveloped in a pall of smoke. But he could see. Drawing back a fold of the wet shawl, he looked at the child. She appeared unharmed. Then he set off running away from the edge of the forest. It was a big park, miles wide. Near the middle there was bare ground. He recognized the place, got his bearings, and made for the point where a deep ravine headed out of this park.

Beyond the bare circle there was more fire, burning sage and grass. His feet were blistered through his boots, and then it seemed he walked on red-hot coals. His clothes caught fire, and he beat it out with bare hands.

Then he stumbled into the rocky ravine. Smoke and blaze above him—the rocks hot—the air suffocating—it was all unendurable. But he kept on. He knew that his strength failed as the conditions bettered. He plunged down, always saving the child when he fell. His sight grew red. Then it grew dark. All was black, or else night had come. He was losing all pain, all sense when he stumbled into water. That saved him. He stayed there. A long time passed till it was light again. His eyes had a thick film over them. Sometimes he could not see at all.

But when he could, he kept on walking, on and on. He knew when he got out of the ravine. He knew where he ought to be. But the smoky gloom obscured everything. He traveled the way he thought he ought to go, and went on and on, endlessly. He did not suffer any more. The weight of the child bore him down. He rested, went on, rested again, went on again till all sense, except a dim sight, failed him. Through that, as in a dream, he saw moving figures, men looming up in the gray fog, hurrying to him.

Far south of the Tonto Range, under the purple shadows of the Peloncillos, there lived a big-hearted rancher with whom Monty Price found a home. He did little odd jobs about the ranch that by courtesy might have been called work. He would never ride a horse again. Monty's legs were warped, his feet hobbled. He did not have free use of his hands. And seldom or never in the presence of any one did he remove his sombrero. For there was not a hair on his head. His face was dark, almost black, with terrible scars.

A burned-out, hobble-footed wreck of a cowboy! but, strangely, there were those at the ranch who learned to love him. They knew his story.

Zane's friends under the Tonto Rim
Zane Grey's West Collection

PARADISE PARK

From *The Man of the Forest* (1919)

Milt Dale is a woodsman who overhears a plot to kidnap two sisters. Milt and his friend, Roy, get to the young women first and lead them to a magical hidden valley where friendly forest creatures and thoughts of love come into the picture. Bo is the younger sister, a beautiful flirt willing to throw caution to the wind. Helen is more mature, a thoughtful beauty.

Travel was arduous. Everywhere were windfalls that had to be avoided, and not a rod was there without a fallen tree. The horses, laboring slowly, sometimes sank knee-deep into the brown duff. Gray moss festooned the tree-trunks and an amber-green moss grew thick on the rotting logs.

Helen loved this forest primeval. It was so still, so dark, so gloomy, so full of shadows and shade, and a dank smell of rotting wood, and sweet fragrance of spruce. The great windfalls, where trees were jammed together in dozens, showed the savagery of the storms. Wherever a single monarch lay uprooted there had sprung up a number of ambitious sons, jealous of one another, fighting for place. Even the trees fought one another! The forest was a place of mystery, but its strife could be read by any eye. The lightning had split firs clear to the roots, and others it had circled with ripping tear from top to trunk.

Time came, however, when the exceeding wildness of the forest, in density and fallen timber, made it imperative for Helen to put all her attention on the ground and trees in her immediate vicinity. So the pleasure of gazing ahead at the beautiful wilderness was denied her. Thereafter travel became toil and the hours endless.

Roy led on, and Ranger followed, while the shadows darkened under the trees. She was reeling in her saddle, half blind and sick, when Roy called out cheerily that they were almost there.

Whatever his idea was, to Helen it seemed many miles that she followed him farther, out of the heavy-timbered forest down upon slopes of low spruce, like evergreen, which descended sharply to another level, where dark, shallow streams flowed gently and the solemn stillness held a low murmur of falling water, and at last the wood ended upon a wonderful park full of a thick, rich, golden light of fast-fading sunset.

"Smell the smoke," said Roy. "By Solomon! if Milt ain't here ahead of me!"

He rode on. Helen's weary gaze took in the round senaca, the circling black slopes, leading up to craggy rims all gold and red in the last flare of the sun; then all the spirit left in her flashed up in thrilling wonder at this exquisite, wild, and colorful spot.

Horses were grazing out in the long grass and there were deer grazing with them. Roy led round a corner of the fringed, bordering woodland, and there, under lofty trees, shone a camp-fire. Huge gray rocks loomed beyond, and then cliffs rose step by step to a notch in the mountain wall, over which poured a thin, lacy waterfall. As Helen gazed in rapture the sunset gold faded to white and all the western slope of the amphitheater darkened.

Dale's tall form appeared.

"Reckon you're late," he said, as with a comprehensive flash of eye he took in the three.

"Milt, I got lost," replied Roy.

"I feared as much.... You girls look like you'd done better to ride with me," went on Dale, as he offered a hand to help Bo off. She took it, tried to get her foot out of the stirrups, and then she slid from the saddle into Dale's arms. He placed her on her feet and, supporting her, said, solicitously: "A hundred-mile ride in three days for a tenderfoot is somethin' your uncle Al won't believe.... Come, walk if it kills you!"

Whereupon he led Bo, very much as if he were teaching a child to walk. The fact that the voluble Bo had nothing to say was significant to Helen, who was following, with the assistance of Roy.

One of the huge rocks resembled a sea-shell in that it contained a hollow over which the wide-spreading shelf flared out. It reached toward branches of great pines. A spring burst from a crack in the solid rock. The campfire blazed under a pine, and the blue column of smoke rose just in front of the shelving rock. Packs were lying on the grass and some of them were open. There were no signs here of a permanent habitation of the hunter. But farther on were other huge rocks, leaning, cracked, and forming caverns, some of which perhaps he utilized.

"My camp is just back," said Dale, as if he had read Helen's mind. "To-morrow we'll fix up comfortable-like round here for you girls."

Helen and Bo were made as easy as blankets and saddles could make them, and the men went about their tasks.

"Nell—isn't this—a dream?" murmured Bo.

"No, child. It's real—terribly real," replied Helen. "Now that we're here—with that awful ride over—we can think."

"Pooh! What difference does that make?... Oh, I don't know which I am—hungrier or tireder!"

"I couldn't eat to-night," said Helen, wearily.

When she stretched out she had a vague, delicious sensation that that was the end of Helen Rayner, and she was glad. Above her, through the lacy, fernlike pine-needles, she saw blue sky and a pale star just showing. Twilight was stealing down swiftly. The silence was beautiful, seemingly undisturbed by the soft, silky, dreamy fall of water. Helen closed her eyes, ready for sleep, with the physical commotion within her body gradually yielding. In some places her bones felt as if they had come out through her flesh; in others throbbed deep-seated aches; her muscles appeared slowly to subside, to relax, with the quivering twinges ceasing one by one; through muscle and bone, through all her body, pulsed a burning current.

Bo's head dropped on Helen's shoulder. Sense became vague to Helen. She lost the low murmur of the waterfall, and then the sound or feeling of someone at the campfire. And her last conscious thought was that she tried to open her eyes and could not.

When she awoke all was bright. The sun shone almost directly overhead. Helen was astounded. Bo lay wrapped in deep sleep, her face flushed, with beads of perspiration on her brow and the chestnut curls damp. Helen threw down the blankets, and then, gathering courage—for she felt as if her back was broken—she endeavored to sit up. In vain! Her spirit was willing, but her muscles refused to act. It must take a violent spasmodic effort. She tried it with shut eyes, and, succeeding, sat there trembling. The commotion she had made in the blankets awoke Bo, and she blinked her surprised blue eyes in the sunlight.

"Hello—Nell! do I have to—get up?" she asked, sleepily.

"Can you?" queried Helen.

"Can I what?" Bo was now thoroughly awake and lay there staring at her sister.

"Why—get up."

"I'd like to know why not," retorted Bo, as she made the effort. She got one arm and shoulder up, only to flop back like a crippled thing. She uttered the most piteous little moan. "I'm dead! I know—I am!"

"Well, if you're going to be a Western girl you'd better have spunk enough to move."

"A-huh!" ejaculated Bo. Then she rolled over, not without groans, and, once upon her face, she raised herself on her hands and turned to a sitting posture. "Where's everybody?... Oh, Nell, it's perfectly lovely here. Paradise!"

Helen looked around. A fire was smoldering. No one was in sight. Wonderful distant colors seemed to strike her glance as she tried to fix it upon near-by objects. A beautiful little green tent or shack had been erected out of spruce boughs. It had a slanting roof that sloped all the way from a ridge-pole to the ground; half of the opening in front was closed, as were the sides. The spruce boughs appeared all to be laid in the same direction, giving it a smooth, compact appearance, actually as if it had grown there.

"That lean-to wasn't there last night?" inquired Bo.

"I didn't see it. Lean-to? Where'd you get that name?"

"It's Western, my dear. I'll bet they put it up for us.... Sure, I see our bags inside. Let's get up. It must be late."

The girls had considerable fun as well as pain in getting up and keeping each other erect until their limbs would hold them firmly. They were delighted with the spruce lean-to. It faced the open and stood just under the wide-spreading shelf of rock. The tiny outlet from the spring flowed beside it and spilled its clear water over a stone, to fall into a little pool. The floor of this woodland habitation consisted of tips of spruce boughs to about a foot in depth, all laid one way, smooth and springy, and so sweetly odorous that the air seemed intoxicating. Helen and Bo opened their baggage, and what with use of the cold water, brush and comb, and clean blouses, they made themselves feel as comfortable as possible, considering the excruciating aches. Then they went out to the campfire.

Helen's eye was attracted by moving objects near at hand. Then simultaneously with Bo's cry of delight Helen saw a beautiful doe approaching under the trees. Dale walked beside it.

"You sure had a long sleep," was the hunter's greeting. "I reckon you both look better."

"Good morning. Or is it afternoon? We're just able to move about," said Helen.

"I could ride," declared Bo, stoutly. "Oh, Nell, look at the deer! It's coming to me."

The doe had hung back a little as Dale reached the camp-fire. It was a gray, slender creature, smooth as silk, with great dark eyes. It stood a moment, long ears erect, and then with a graceful little trot came up to Bo and reached a slim nose for her outstretched hand. All about it, except the beautiful soft eyes, seemed wild, and yet it was as tame as a kitten. Then, suddenly, as Bo fondled the long ears, it gave a start and, breaking away, ran back out of sight under the pines.

"What frightened it?" asked Bo.

Dale pointed up at the wall under the shelving roof of rock. There, twenty feet from the ground, curled up on a ledge, lay a huge tawny animal with a face like that of a cat.

"She's afraid of Tom," replied Dale. "Recognizes him as a hereditary foe, I guess. I can't make friends of them."

"Oh! So that's Tom—the pet lion!" exclaimed Bo. "Ugh! No wonder that deer ran off!"

"How long has he been up there?" queried Helen, gazing fascinated at Dale's famous pet.

"I couldn't say. Tom comes an' goes," replied Dale. "But I sent him up there last night."

"And he was there—perfectly free—right over us—while we slept!" burst out Bo.

"Yes. An' I reckon you slept the safer for that."

"Of all things! Nell, isn't he a monster? But he doesn't look like a lion—an African lion. He's a panther. I saw his like at the circus once."

"He's a cougar," said Dale. "The panther is long and slim. Tom is not only long, but thick an' round. I've had him four years. An' he was a kitten no bigger 'n my fist when I got him."

"Is he perfectly tame—safe?" asked Helen, anxiously.

"I've never told anybody that Tom was safe, but he is," replied Dale. "You can absolutely believe it. A wild cougar wouldn't attack a man unless cornered or starved. An' Tom is like a big kitten."

The beast raised his great catlike face, with its sleepy, half-shut eyes, and looked down upon them.

"Shall I call him down?" inquired Dale.

For once Bo did not find her voice.

"Let us—get a little more used to him—at a distance," replied Helen, with a little laugh.

"If he comes to you, just rub his head an' you'll see how tame he is," said Dale. "Reckon you're both hungry?"

"Not so very," returned Helen, aware of his penetrating gray gaze upon her.

"Well, I am," vouchsafed Bo.

"Soon as the turkey's done we'll eat. My camp is round between the rocks. I'll call you."

Not until his broad back was turned did Helen notice that the hunter looked different. Then she saw he wore a lighter, cleaner suit of buckskin, with no coat, and instead of the high-heeled horseman's boots he wore moccasins and leggings. The change made him appear more lithe.

"Nell, I don't know what you think, but *I* call him handsome," declared Bo.

Helen had no idea what she thought.

"Let's try to walk some," she suggested.

So they essayed that painful task and got as far as a pine log some few rods from their camp. This point was close to the edge of the park, from which there was an unobstructed view.

"My! What a place!" exclaimed Bo, with eyes wide and round.

"Oh, beautiful!" breathed Helen.

An unexpected blaze of color drew her gaze first. Out of the black spruce slopes shone patches of aspens, gloriously red and gold, and low down along the edge of timber troops of aspens ran out into the park, not yet so blazing as those above, but purple and yellow and white in the sunshine. Masses of silver spruce, like trees in moonlight, bordered the park, sending out here and there an isolated tree, sharp as a spear, with under-branches close to the ground. Long golden-green grass, resembling half-ripe wheat, covered the entire floor of the park, gently waving to the wind. Above sheered the black, gold-patched slopes, steep and unscalable, rising to buttresses of dark, iron-hued rock. And to the east circled the rows of cliff-bench, gray and old and fringed, splitting at the top in the notch where the lacy, slumberous waterfall, like white smoke, fell and vanished, to reappear in wider sheet of lace, only to fall and vanish again in the green depths.

It was a verdant valley, deep-set in the mountain walls, wild and sad and lonesome. The waterfall dominated the spirit of the place, dreamy and sleepy and tranquil; it murmured sweetly on one breath of wind, and lulled with another, and sometimes died out altogether, only to come again in soft, strange roar.

"Paradise Park!" whispered Bo to herself.

A call from Dale disturbed their raptures. Turning, they hobbled with eager but painful steps in the direction of a larger camp-fire, situated to the right of the great rock that sheltered their lean-to. No hut or house showed there and none was needed. Hiding-places and homes for a hundred hunters were there in the sections of caverned cliffs, split off in bygone ages from the mountain wall above. A few stately pines stood out from the rocks, and a clump of silver spruce ran down to a brown brook.

This camp was only a step from the lean-to, round the corner of a huge rock, yet it had been out of sight. Here indeed was evidence of a hunter's home—pelts and skins and antlers, a neat pile of split fire-wood, a long ledge of rock, well sheltered, and loaded with bags like a huge pantry-shelf, packs and ropes and saddles, tools and weapons, and a platform of dry brush as shelter for a fire around which hung on poles a various assortment of utensils for camp.

"Hyar—you git!" shouted Dale, and he threw a stick at something. A bear cub scampered away in haste. He was small and woolly and brown, and he grunted as he ran. Soon he halted.

"That's Bud," said Dale, as the girls came up. "Guess he near starved in my absence. An' now he wants everythin', especially the sugar. We don't have sugar often up here."

"Isn't he dear? Oh, I love him!" cried Bo. "Come back, Bud. Come, Buddie."

The cub, however, kept his distance, watching Dale with bright little eyes.

"You may have to stay here with me—for weeks—maybe months— if we've the bad luck to get snowed in," he said, slowly, as if startled at this deduction. "You're safe here. There's plenty to eat an' it's a pretty place."

"Pretty! Why, it's grand!" exclaimed Bo. "I've called it Paradise Park."

"Paradise Park," he repeated, weighing the words. "You've named it an' also the creek. Paradise Creek! I've been here twelve years with no fit name for my home till you said that."

"Oh, that pleases me!" returned Bo, with shining eyes.

"Eat now," said Dale. "An' I reckon you'll like that turkey."

There was a clean tarpaulin upon which were spread steaming, fragrant pans—roast turkey, hot biscuits and gravy, mashed potatoes as white as if prepared at home, stewed dried apples, and butter and coffee. This bounteous repast surprised and delighted the girls; when they had once tasted the roast wild turkey, then Milt Dale had occasion to blush at their encomiums.

"I hope—Uncle Al—doesn't come for a month," declared Bo, as she tried to get her breath.

There was a brown spot on her nose and one on each cheek, suspiciously close to her mouth.

Dale laughed. It was pleasant to hear him, for his laugh seemed unused and deep, as if it came from tranquil depths.

"Won't you eat with us?" asked Helen.

"Reckon I will," he said, "it'll save time, an' hot grub tastes better."

Quite an interval of silence ensued, which presently was broken by Dale.

"Here comes Tom."

Helen observed with a thrill that the cougar was magnificent, seen erect on all-fours, approaching with slow, sinuous grace. His color was tawny, with spots of whitish gray. He had bow-legs, big and round and furry, and a huge head with great tawny eyes. No matter how tame he was said to be, he looked wild. Like a dog he walked right up, and it so happened that he was directly behind Bo, within reach of her when she turned.

"Oh, Lord!" cried Bo, and up went both of her hands, in one of which was a huge piece of turkey. Tom took it, not viciously, but nevertheless with a snap that made Helen jump. As if by magic the turkey vanished. And Tom took a closer step toward Bo. Her expression of fright changed to consternation.

"He stole my turkey!"

"Tom, come here," ordered Dale, sharply. The cougar glided round rather sheepishly. "Now lie down an' behave."

Tom crouched on all-fours, his head resting on his paws, with his beautiful tawny eyes, light and piercing, fixed upon the hunter.

"Don't grab," said Dale, holding out a piece of turkey. Whereupon Tom took it less voraciously.

As it happened, the little bear cub saw this transaction, and he plainly indicated his opinion of the preference shown to Tom.

"Oh, the dear!" exclaimed Bo. "He means it's not fair.... Come, Bud—come on."

But Bud would not approach the group until called by Dale. Then he scrambled to them with every manifestation of delight. Bo almost forgot her own needs in feeding him and getting acquainted with him. Tom plainly showed his jealousy of Bud, and Bud likewise showed his fear of the great cat.

Helen could not believe the evidence of her eyes—that she was in the woods calmly and hungrily partaking of sweet, wild-flavored meat— that a full-grown mountain lion lay on one side of her and a baby brown bear sat on the other—that a strange hunter, a man of the forest, there in his lonely and isolated fastness, appealed to the romance in her and interested her as no one else she had ever met.

When the wonderful meal was at last finished Bo enticed the bear cub around to the camp of the girls, and there soon became great comrades with him. Helen, watching Bo play, was inclined to envy her. No matter where Bo was placed, she always got something out of it. She adapted herself. She, who could have a good time with almost anyone or anything, would find the hours sweet and fleeting in this beautiful park of wild wonders.

But merely objective actions—merely physical movements, had never yet contented Helen. She could run and climb and ride and play with hearty and healthy abandon, but those things would not suffice long for her, and her mind needed food. Helen was a thinker. One reason she had desired to make her home in the West was that by taking up a life of the open, of action, she might think and dream and brood less. And here she was in the wild West, after the three most strenuously active days of her career, and still the same old giant revolved her mind and turned it upon herself and upon all she saw.

"What can I do?" she asked Bo, almost helplessly.

"Why, rest, you silly!" retorted Bo. "You walk like an old, crippled woman with only one leg."

Helen hoped the comparison was undeserved, but the advice was sound. The blankets spread out on the grass looked inviting and they felt comfortably warm in the sunshine. The breeze was slow, languorous, fragrant, and it brought the low hum of the murmuring waterfall, like a melody of bees. Helen made a pillow and lay down to rest. The green pine-needles, so thin and fine in their crisscross network, showed clearly against the blue sky. She looked in vain for birds. Then her gaze went wonderingly to the lofty fringed rim of the great amphitheater, and as she studied it she began to grasp its remoteness, how far away it was in the rarefied atmosphere. A black eagle, sweeping along, looked of tiny size, and yet he was far under the heights above. How pleasant she fancied it to be up there! And drowsy fancy lulled her to sleep.

Helen slept all afternoon, and upon awakening, toward sunset, found Bo curled beside her. Dale had thoughtfully covered them with a blanket; also he had built a camp-fire. The air was growing keen and cold.

Later, when they had put their coats on and made comfortable seats beside the fire, Dale came over, apparently to visit them.

"I reckon you can't sleep all the time," he said. "An' bein' city girls, you'll get lonesome."

"Lonesome!" echoed Helen. The idea of her being lonesome here had not occurred to her.

"I've thought that all out," went on Dale, as he sat down, Indian fashion, before the blaze. "It's natural you'd find time drag up here, bein' used to lots of people an' goin's-on, an' work, an' all girls like."

"I'd never be lonesome here," replied Helen, with her direct force.

Dale did not betray surprise, but he showed that his mistake was something to ponder over.

"Excuse me," he said, presently, as his gray eyes held hers. "That's how I had it. As I remember girls—an' it doesn't seem long since I left home—most of them would die of lonesomeness up here." Then he addressed himself to Bo. "How about you? You see, I figured you'd be the one that liked it, an' your sister the one who wouldn't."

"I won't get lonesome very soon," replied Bo.

"I'm glad. It worried me some—not ever havin' girls as company before. An' in a day or so, when you're rested, I'll help you pass the time."

Bo's eyes were full of flashing interest, and Helen asked him, "How?"

It was a sincere expression of her curiosity and not doubtful or ironic challenge of an educated woman to a man of the forest. But as a challenge he took it.

"How!" he repeated, and a strange smile flitted across his face. "Why, by givin' you rides an' climbs to beautiful places. An' then, if you're interested,' to show you how little so-called civilized people know of nature."

Helen realized then that whatever his calling, hunter or wanderer or hermit, he was not uneducated, even if he appeared illiterate.

"I'll be happy to learn from you," she said.

"Me, too!" chimed in Bo. "You can't tell too much to any one from Missouri."

He smiled, and that warmed Helen to him, for then he seemed less removed from other people. About this hunter there began to be something of the very nature of which he spoke—a stillness, aloofness, an unbreakable tranquility, a cold, clear spirit like that in the mountain air, a physical something not unlike the tamed wildness of his pets or the strength of the pines.

"I'll bet I can tell you more 'n you'll ever remember," he said.

"What 'll you bet?" retorted Bo.

"Well, more roast turkey against—say somethin' nice when you're safe an' home to your uncle Al's, runnin' his ranch."

"Agreed. Nell, you hear?"

Helen nodded her head.

"All right. We'll leave it to Nell," began Dale, half seriously. "Now I'll tell you, first, for the fun of passin' time we'll ride an' race my horses out in the park. An' we'll fish in the brooks an' hunt in the woods. There's an old silvertip around that you can see me kill. An' we'll climb to the peaks an' see wonderful sights.... So much for that. Now, if you really want to learn—or if you only want me to tell you—well, that's no matter. Only I'll win the bet! You'll see how this park lies in the crater of a volcano an' was once full of water—an' how the snow blows in on one side in winter, a hundred feet deep, when there's none on the other. An' the trees—how they grow an' live an' fight one another an' depend on one another, an' protect the forest from storm-winds. An' how they hold the water that is the fountains of the great rivers. An' how the creatures an' things that live in them or on them are good for them, an' neither could live without the other. An' then I'll show you my pets tame an' untamed, an' tell you how it's man that makes any creature wild—how easy they are to tame—an' how they learn to love you. An' there's the life of the forest, the strife of it—how the bear lives, an' the cats, an' the wolves, an' the deer. You'll see how cruel nature is how savage an' wild the wolf or cougar tears down the deer—how a wolf loves fresh, hot blood, an' how a cougar unrolls the skin of a deer back from his neck. An' you'll see that this cruelty of nature—this work of the wolf an' cougar—is what makes the deer so beautiful an' healthy an' swift an' sensitive. Without his deadly foes the deer would deteriorate an' die out. An' you'll see how this principle works out among all creatures of the forest. Strife! It's the meanin' of all creation, an' the salvation. If you're quick to see, you'll learn that the nature here in the wilds is the same as that of men—only men are no longer cannibals. Trees fight to live—birds fight—animals fight—men fight. They all live off one another. An' it's this fightin' that brings them all closer an' closer to bein' perfect. But nothin' will ever be perfect."

"But how about religion?" interrupted Helen, earnestly.

"Nature has a religion, an' it's to live—to grow—to reproduce, each of its kind."

"But that is not God or the immortality of the soul," declared Helen.

"Well, it's as close to God an' immortality as nature ever gets."

"Oh, you would rob me of my religion!"

"No, I just talk as I see life," replied Dale, reflectively, as he poked a stick into the red embers of the fire. "Maybe I have a religion. I don't know. But it's not the kind you have—not the Bible kind. That kind doesn't keep the men in Pine an' Snowdrop an' all over—sheepmen an' ranchers an' farmers an' travelers, such as I've known—the religion they profess doesn't keep them from lyin', cheatin', stealin', an' killin'. I reckon no man who lives as I do—which perhaps is my religion—will lie or cheat or steal or kill, unless it's to kill in self-defense. My religion, maybe, is love of life—wild life as it was in the beginnin'—an' the wind that blows secrets from everywhere, an' the water that sings all day an' night, an' the stars that shine constant, an' the trees that speak somehow, an' the rocks that aren't dead. I'm never alone here or on the trails. There's somethin' unseen, but always with me. An' that's It! Call it God if you like. But what stalls me is—where was that Spirit when this earth was a ball of fiery gas? Where will that Spirit be when all life is frozen out or burned out on this globe an' it hangs dead in space like the moon? That time will come. There's no waste in nature. Not the littlest atom is destroyed. It changes, that's all, as you see this pine wood go up in smoke an' feel somethin' that's heat come out of it. Where does that go? It's not lost. Nothin' is lost. So, the beautiful an' savin' thought is, maybe all rock an' wood, water an' blood an' flesh, are resolved back into the elements, to come to life somewhere again sometime."

"Oh, what you say is wonderful, but it's terrible!" exclaimed Helen. He had struck deep into her soul.

"Terrible? I reckon," he replied, sadly.

Then ensued a little interval of silence.

"Milt Dale, I lose the bet," declared Bo, with earnestness behind her frivolity.

"I'd forgotten that. Reckon I talked a lot," he said, apologetically. "You see, I don't get much chance to talk, except to myself or Tom. Years ago, when I found the habit of silence settlin' down on me, I took to thinkin' out loud an' talkin' to anythin'."

"I could listen to you all night," returned Bo, dreamily.

"Do you read—do you have books?" inquired Helen, suddenly.

"Yes, I read tolerable well; a good deal better than I talk or write," he replied. "I went to school till I was fifteen. Always hated study, but liked to read. Years ago an old friend of mine down here at Pine— Widow Cass—she gave me a lot of old books. An' I packed them up here. Winter's the time I read."

Conversation lagged after that, except for desultory remarks, and presently Dale bade the girls good night and left them. Helen watched his tall form vanish in the gloom under the pines, and after he had disappeared she still stared.

"Nell!" called Bo, shrilly. "I've called you three times. I want to go to bed."

"Oh! I—I was thinking," rejoined Helen, half embarrassed, half wondering at herself. "I didn't hear you."

"I should smile you didn't," retorted Bo. "Wish you could just have seen your eyes. Nell, do you want me to tell you something?"

"Why—yes," said Helen, rather feebly. She did not like it at all, when Bo talked like that.

"You're going to fall in love with that wild hunter," declared Bo in a voice that rang like a bell.

Helen was not only amazed, but enraged. She caught her breath preparatory to giving this incorrigible sister a piece of her mind. Bo went calmly on.

"I can feel it in my bones."

"Bo, you're a little fool—a sentimental, romancing, gushy little fool!" retorted Helen. "All you seem to hold in your head is some rot about love. To hear you talk one would think there's nothing else in the world but love."

Bo's eyes were bright, shrewd, affectionate, and laughing as she bent their steady gaze upon Helen.

"Nell, that's just it. There *is* nothing else!"

Zane Grey's West Society Collection

Zane Grey's West Society Collection

**Zane Grey holding a black bass
with his brother, Reddy**
Upper Delaware Scenic and Recreational River,
National Park Service, Zane Grey Museum.

THE LORD
OF LACKAWAXEN CREEK

Outing Magazine (May 1909)

Zane Grey and his wife, Dolly, lived and raised their family in Lackawaxen, Pennsylvania for many years. This real life story is about Zane and his brother, Reddy, fishing not far from home. If you like this story, you might buy Zane Grey's Tales of Freshwater Fishing, *which has a lot more like it.*

Winding among the Blue Hills of Pennsylvania there is a swift amber stream that the Indians named Lack-a-wax-en. The literal translation no one seems to know, but it must mean, in mystical and imaginative Delaware, "the brown water that turns and whispers and tumbles." It is a little river hidden away under gray cliffs and hills black with ragged pines. It is full of mossy stones and rapid ripples.

All its tributaries, dashing white-sheeted over ferny cliffs, wine-brown where the whirling pools suck the stain from the hemlock root, harbor the speckled trout. Wise in their generation, the black and red-spotted little beauties keep to their brooks; for, farther down, below the rush and fall, a newcomer is lord of the stream. He is an archenemy, a scorner of beauty and blood, the wolf-jawed, red-eyed, bronze-backed black bass.

A mile or more from its mouth the Lackawaxen leaves the shelter of the hills and seeks the open sunlight and slows down to widen into long lanes that glide reluctantly over the few last restraining barriers to the Delaware. In a curve between two of these level lanes, there is a place where barefoot boys wade and fish for chubs and bask on the big boulders like turtles. It is a famous hole of chubs and bright-sided shiners and sunfish. And, perhaps because it is so known, and so shallow, so open to the sky, few fishermen ever learned that in its secret stony caverns hid a great golden-bronze treasure of a bass.

In vain had many a flimsy feathered hook been flung over his lair by fly casters and whisked gracefully across the gilding surface of his pool. In vain had many a shiny spoon and pearly minnow reflected sun glints through the watery windows of his home. In vain had many a hellgrammite and frog and grasshopper been dropped in front of his broad nose.

Chance plays the star part on a fisherman's luck. One still, cloudy day, when the pool glanced dark under a leaden sky, I saw a wave that reminded me of the wake of a rolling tarpon; then followed an angry swirl, the skitter of a frantically leaping chub, and a splash that ended with a sound like the deep chung of water sharply turned by an oar.

Big bass choose strange hiding places. They should be looked for in just such holes and rifts and shallows as will cover their backs. But to corral a six-pounder in the boys' swimming hole was a circumstance to temper a fisherman's vanity with experience.

Thrillingly conscious of the possibilities of this pool, I studied it thoughtfully. It was a wide, shallow bend in the stream, with dark channels between submerged rocks, suggestive of underlying shelves. It had a current, too, not noticeable at first glance. And this pool looked at long and carefully, colored by the certainty of its guardian, took on an aspect most alluring to an angler's spirit. It had changed from a pond girt by stony banks, to a foam-flecked running stream, clear, yet hiding its secrets, shallow, yet full of labyrinthine watercourses. It presented problems which, difficult as they were, faded in a breath before a fisherman's optimism.

I tested my leader, changed the small hook for a large one, and selecting a white shiner fully six inches long, I lightly hooked it through the side of the upper lip. A sensation never outgrown since boyhood, a familiar mingling of strange fear and joyous anticipation, made me stoop low and tread the slippery stones as if I were a stalking Indian. I knew that a glimpse of me or a faint jar vibrating under the water, or an unnatural ripple on its surface, would be fatal to my enterprise.

I swung the lively minnow and instinctively dropped it with a splash over a dark space between two yellow sunken stones. Out of the amber depths started a broad bar of bronze, rose and flashed into gold. A little dimpling eddying circle, most fascinating of all watery forms, appeared round where the minnow had sunk. The golden moving flash went down and vanished in the greenish gloom like a tiger stealing into a jungle. The line trembled, slowly swept out and straightened. How fraught that instant with a wild yet waiting suspense, with a thrill potent and blissful!

Did the fisherman ever live who could wait in such a moment? My arms twitched involuntarily. Then I struck hard, but not half hard enough. The bass leaped out of a flying splash, shook himself in a tussle plainly audible, and slung the hook back at me like a bullet.

In such moments one never sees the fish distinctly; excitement deranges the vision, and the picture, though impressive, is dim and dreamlike. But a blind man would have known this bass to be enormous, for when he fell he cut the water as a heavy stone.

The best of fishing is that a mild philosophy attends even the greatest misfortunes. It is a delusion peculiar to fishermen, and I went on my way upstream, cheerfully, as one who minded not at all an incident of angling practice; spiritedly, as one who had seen many a big bass go by the board. I found myself thinking about my two brothers, Cedar and Reddy for short, both anglers of longstanding and some reputation. It was a sore point with me and a stock subject for endless disputes that they could never appreciate my superiority as a fisherman. Brothers are singularly prone to such points of view. So when I thought of them I felt the incipient stirring of a mighty plot. It occurred to me that the iron-mouthed old bass, impregnable of jaw as well as of stronghold, might be made to serve a turn. And all the afternoon the thing grew and grew in my mind.

Luck otherwise favored me, and I took home a fair string of fish. I remarked to my brothers that the conditions for fishing the stream were favorable. Thereafter morning on morning my eyes sought the heavens, appealing for a cloudy day. At last one came, and I invited Reddy to go with me. With childish pleasure that would have caused weakness in any but an unscrupulous villain, he eagerly accepted. He looked over a great assortment of tackle, and finally selected a five-ounce Leonard bait rod carrying a light reel and fine line. When I thought of what would happen if Reddy hooked that powerful bass, an unholy glee fastened upon my soul.

We never started out that way together, swinging rods and pails, but old associations were awakened. We called up the time when we had left the imprints of bare feet on the country roads; we lived over many a boyhood adventure by a running stream. And at last we wound up on the never threadbare question as to the merit and use of tackle.

"I always claimed," said Reddy, "that a fisherman should choose tackle for a day's work after the fashion of a hunter in choosing his gun. A hunter knows what kind of game he's after, and takes a small or large caliber accordingly. Of course a fisherman has more rods than there are calibers of guns, but the rule holds. Now today I have brought this light rod and thin line because I don't need weight. I don't see why you've brought that heavy rod. Even a two-pound bass would be a great surprise up this stream."

"You're right," I replied, "but I sort of lean to possibilities. Besides I'm fond of this rod. You know I've caught a half dozen bass of from five to six pounds with it. I wonder what you would do if you hooked a big one on your delicate rod."

"Do?" exclaimed my brother. "I'd have a fit! I might handle a big bass in deep water with this outfit, but here in this shallow stream with its rocks and holes I couldn't. And that is the reason so few big bass are taken from the Delaware. We know they are there, great lusty fellows! Every day in season we hear some tale of woe from some fisherman. Hooked a big one-broke this-broke that-got under a stone. That's why no five- or six-pound bass are taken from shallow, swift, rock-bedded streams on light tackle."

When we reached the pool I sat down and began to fumble with my leader. How generously I let Reddy have the first cast! My iniquity carried me to the extreme of bidding him steal softly and stoop low. I saw a fat chub swinging in the air; I saw it alight to disappear in a churning commotion of the water, and I heard Reddy's startled, "Gee!"

Hard upon his exclamation followed action of striking swiftness. A shrieking reel, willow wand of a rod wavering like a buggy whip in the wind, curving splashes round a foam-lashed swell, a crack of dry wood, a sound as of a banjo string snapping, a sharp splash, then a heavy sullen souse; these, with Reddy standing voiceless, eyes glaring on the broken rod and limp trailing line, were the essentials of the tragedy.

Somehow the joke did not ring true when Reddy waded ashore calm and self-contained, with only his burning eyes to show how deeply he felt. What he said to me in a quiet voice must not, owing to family pride, go on record. It most assuredly would not be an addition to the fish literature of the day.

But he never mentioned the incident to Cedar, which omission laid the way open for my further machinations. I realized that I should have tried Cedar first. He was one of those white-duck-pants-on-a-dry-rock sort of a fisherman, anyway. And in due time I had him wading out toward the center of that pool.

I always experienced a painful sensation while watching Cedar cast. One moment he resembled Ajax defying the lightning and the next he looked like the fellow who stood on a monument, smiling at grief. Cedar's execution was wonderful. I have seen him cast a frog a mile- but the frog had left the hook. It was remarkable to see him catch his hat, and terrifying to hear the language he used at such an ordinary angling event.

It was not safe to be in his vicinity, but if this was unavoidable, the better course was to face him; because if you turned your back an instant, his flying hook would have a fiendish affinity for your trousers, and it was not beyond his powers to swing you kicking out over the stream. All of which, considering the frailties of human nature and of fishermen, could be forgiven; he had, however, one great fault impossible to over-look, and it was that he made more noise than a playful hippopotamus. I hoped, despite all these things, that the big bass would rise to the occasion. He did rise. He must have recognized the situation of his life. He spread the waters of his shallow pool and accommodatingly hooked himself.

Cedar's next graceful move was to fall off the slippery stone on which he had been standing and to go out of sight. His hat floated downstream; the arched tip of his rod came up, then his arm, and his dripping shoulders and body. He yelled like a savage and pulled on the fish hard enough to turn a tuna in the air. The big bass leaped three times, made a long shoot with his black dorsal fin showing, and then, with a lunge, headed for some place remote from there. Cedar plowed after him, sending the water in sheets, and then he slipped, wildly swung his arms, and fell again.

I was sinking to the ground, owing to unutterable and overpowering sensations of joy, when a yell and a commotion in the bushes heralded the appearance of Reddy.

"Hang on, Cedar! Hang on! " he cried, and began an Indian war dance.

The few succeeding moments were somewhat blurred because of my excess of motion. When I returned to consciousness, Cedar was wading out with a hookless leader, a bloody shin, and a disposition utterly and irretrievably ruined.

"Put a job on me!" he roared.

Thereafter during the summer each of us made solitary and sneaking expeditions, bent on the capture of the lord of the Lackawaxen. And somehow each would return to find the other two derisively speculative as to what caused his clouded brow. Leader on leader went to grace the rocks of the old bronze warrior's home. At length Cedar and Reddy gave up, leaving the pool to me. I fed more than one choice shiner to the bass and more than once he sprang into the air to return my hook.

Summer and autumn passed; winter came to lock the Lackawaxen in icy fetters; I fished under Southern skies where lagoons and moss-shaded waters teemed with great and gamy fish, but I never forgot him. I knew that when the season rolled around, when a June sun warmed the cold spring-fed Lackawaxen, he would be waiting for me.

Who was it spoke of the fleeting of time? Obviously he had never waited for the opening of the fishing season. At last the tedious time, like the water, flowed by. But then I found I had another long wait. Brilliant June days without a cloud were a joy to live, but worthless for fishing. Through all that beautiful month I plodded up to the pool, only to be unrewarded. Doubt began to assail me. Might not the ice, during the spring break-up, have scared him from the shallow hole? No. I felt that not even a rolling glacier could have moved him from his subterranean home.

Often as I reached the pool I saw fishermen wading down the stream, and on these occasions I sat on the bank and lazily waited for the intruders to pass on. Once, the first time I saw them, I had an agonizing fear that one of the yellow-helmeted, khaki-coated anglers would hook my bass. The fear, of course, was groundless. The idea of that grand fish rising to a feathery imitation of a bug or a lank dead bait had nothing in my experience to warrant its consideration.

Small, lively bass, full of play, fond of chasing their golden shadows, and belligerent and hungry, were ready to fight and eat whatever swam into their ken. But a six-pound bass, slow to reach such weight in swift-running water, was old and wise and full of years. He did not feed often, and when he did he wanted a live fish big enough for a good mouthful. So, with these facts to soothe me I rested my fears, and got to look humorously at the invasions of the summer-hotel fishers.

They came wading, slipping, splashing downstream, blowing like porpoises, slapping at the water with all kinds of artificial and dead bait. And they called to me in a humor inspired by my fishing garb and the rustic environment:

"Hey, Rube! Ketchin' any?"

I said the suckers were bitin' right pert.

"What d'you call this stream?"

I replied, giving the Indian name.

"Lack-a-what? Can't you whistle it? Lack-awhacken? You mean Lack-afishin'."

"Lack-arotten," joined in another.

"Do you live here?" questioned a third.

I said yes.

"Why don't you move?" Whereupon they all laughed and pursued the noisy tenor of their way downstream, pitching their baits around.

"Say, fellows," I shouted after them, "are you training for the casting tournament in Madison Square Garden or do you think you're playing lacrosse?"

The laugh that came back proved the joke on them, and that it would be remembered as part of the glorious time they were having.

July brought the misty, dark, lowering days. Not only did I find the old king at home on these days, but just as contemptuous of hooks and leaders as he had been the summer before. About the middle of the month he stopped giving me paralysis of the heart; that is to say, he quit rising to my tempting chums and shiners. So I left him alone to rest, to rust out hooks and grow less suspicious.

By the time August came, the desire to call on him again was well-nigh irresistible. But I waited, and fished the Delaware, and still waited. I would get him when the harvest moon was full. Like all the old moss-backed denizens of the shady holes, he would come out then for a last range over the feeding shoals.

At length a morning broke humid and warm, almost dark as twilight, with little gusts of fine rain. Of all days this was the day! I chose a stiff rod, a heavy silk line, a stout brown leader, and a large hook. From my bait box I took two five-inch red catfish, the little "stone-rollers" of the Delaware, and several long shiners. Thus equipped, I sallied forth.

The walk up the towpath, along the canal with its rushes and sedges, across the meadows white with late-blooming daisies, lost nothing because of its familiarity. When I reached the pool I saw in the low water near shore several small bass scouting among the schools of minnows. I did not want these pugnacious fellows to kill my bait, so, procuring a hellgrammite from under a stone, I put it on my hook and promptly caught two of them, and gave the other a scare he would not soon forget.

I decided to try the bass with one of his favorite shiners. With this trailing in the water I silently waded out, making not so much as a ripple. The old familiar oppression weighed on my breast; the old throbbing boyish excitement tingled through my blood.

I made a long cast and dropped the shiner lightly. He went under and then came up to swim about on the surface. This was a sign that made my heart leap. Then the water bulged, and a black bar shot across the middle of the long shiner. He went down out of sight, the last gleams of his divided brightness fading slowly. I did not need to see the little shower of silver scales floating up to know that the black bar had been the rounded nose of the old bass and that he had taken the shiner across the middle. I struck hard, and my hook came whistling at me. I had scored a clean miss.

I waded ashore very carefully, sat down on a stone by my bait pail, and meditated. Would he rise again? I had never known him to do so twice in one day. But then there had never been occasion. I thought of the "stone-rollers" and thrilled with certainty. Whatever he might resist, he could not resist one of those little red catfish. Long ago, when he was only a three- or four-pounder, roaming the deep eddies and swift rapids of the Delaware, before he had isolated himself to a peaceful old age in this quiet pool, he must have poked his nose under many a stone, with red eyes keen for one of those dainty morsels.

My excitation thrilled itself out to the calm assurance of the experienced fisherman. I firmly fastened on one of the catfish and stole out into the pool. I waded farther than ever before; I was careful but confident. Then I saw the two flat rocks dimly shining. The water was dark as it rippled by, gurgling softly; it gleamed with lengthening shadows and glints of amber.

I swung the catfish. A dull flash of sunshine seemed to come up to meet him. The water swirled and broke with a splash. The broad black head of the bass just skimmed the surface; his jaws opened wide to take in the bait; he turned and flapped a huge spread tail on the water.

Then I struck with all the power the tackle would stand. I felt the hook catch solidly as if in a sunken log. Swift as flashing light the bass leaped. The drops of water hissed and the leader whizzed. But the hook held. I let out one exultant yell.

He did not leap again. He dashed to the right, then the left, in bursts of surprising speed. I had hardly warmed to the work when he settled down and made for the dark channel between the yellow rocks. My triumph was to be short-lived. Where was the beautiful spectacular surface fight I expected of him? Cunning old monarch! He laid his great weight dead on the line and lunged for his sunken throne. I held him with a grim surety of the impossibility of stopping him. How I longed for deep, open water! The rod bent, the line strained and stretched. I removed my thumb and the reel sang one short shrill song. Then the bass was as still as the rock under which he had gone.

I had never dislodged a big bass from under a stone, and I saw herein further defeat; but I persevered, wading to different angles, and working all the tricks of the trade. I could not drag the fish out, nor pull the hook loose. I sat down on a stone and patiently waited for a long time, hoping he would come out on his own accord.

As a final resort I waded out. The water rose to my waist, then to my shoulders, my chin, and all but covered my raised face. When I reached the stone under which he had planted himself, I stood in water about four feet deep. I saw my leader, and tugged upon it, and kicked under the stone, all to no good.

Then I calculated I had a chance to dislodge him if I could get my arm under the shelf. So I went, hat, rod, and all. The current was just swift enough to lift my feet, making my task most difficult. At the third trial I got my hand on a sharp corner of stone and held fast. I ran my right hand along the leader, under the projecting slab of rock, till I touched the bass. I tried to get hold of him, but had to rise for air.

I dove again. The space was narrow, so narrow that I wondered how so large a fish could have gotten there. He had gone under sidewise, turned, and wedged his dorsal fin, fixing himself as solidly as the rock itself. I pulled frantically till I feared I would break the leader.

When I floundered up to breathe again, the thought occurred to me that I could rip him with my knife and, by taking the life out of him, loosen the powerful fin so he could be dragged out. Still, much as I wanted him, I could not do that. I resolved to make one more fair attempt. In a quick determined plunge I secured a more favor-able hold for my left hand and reached under with my right. I felt his whole long length and I could not force a finger behind him anywhere. The gill toward me was shut tight like a trap door. But I got a thumb and forefinger fastened to his lip. I tugged till a severe cramp numbed my hand; I saw red and my head whirled; a noise roared in my ears. I stayed until one more second would have made me a drowning man, then rose gasping and choking.

I broke off the leader close to the stone and waded ashore. I looked back at the pool, faintly circled by widening ripples. What a great hole and what a grand fish! I was glad I did not get him and knew I would never again disturb his peace.

So I took my rod and pail and the two little bass, and brushed the meadow daisies, and threaded the familiar green-lined towpath toward home.

Ken cutting a crocodile loose
Illustration by Victor Clyde Forsythe,
Ken Ward in the Jungle, 1912

CROCODILE DAY

Condensed from *Ken Ward in the Jungle* (1912)

If you read "Ken and Hal Meet the Mountain Lions", you are likely to enjoy this brief story as well. It's from another book by Zane Grey called Ken Ward in the Jungle. *In this story, Ken and Hal travel down a jungle river near Tampico, Mexico, and nearly become supper for some huge crocodiles.*

It must have been late, for the moon was low. Ken was falling asleep when the clink of tin pans made him sit up with a start. Some animal was prowling about camp. He peered into the moonlit shadows, but could make out no unfamiliar object. Still he was not satisfied; so he awoke Pepe.

Certainly it was not Ken's intention to let Pepe get out ahead; nevertheless, before he started, Pepe rolled out of the tent.

"Santa Maria!" shrieked Pepe.

Ken fumbled under his pillow for a gun. Hal raised up so quickly that he bumped Ken's head, making him see a million stars. George rolled over, nearly knocking down the tent.

From outside came a sliddery, rustling noise, then another yell that was deadened by a sounding splash. Ken leaped out with his gun, George at his elbow. Pepe stood just back of the tent, his arms upraised, and he appeared stunned. The water near the bank was boiling and bubbling; waves were dashing on the shore and ripples spreading in a circle.

George shouted in Spanish.

"Crocodile!" cried Ken.

"Si, si, Senor," replied Pepe. Then he said that when he stepped out of the tent the crocodile was right in camp, not ten feet from where the boys lay. Pepe also said that these brutes were man-eaters, and that he had better watch for the rest of the night. Ken thought him inclined to exaggerate; however, he made no objection to Pepe's holding watch over the crocodile.

By nine o'clock they were packed, and, turning into the shady channel, soon were out in the sunlight saying good-by to Cypress Island. They turned a curve to run under a rocky bluff from which came a muffled roar of rapids. A long, projecting point of rock extended across the river, allowing the water to rush through only at a narrow mill-race channel close to the shore. It was an obstacle to get around.

There was no possibility of lifting the boat over the bridge of rock, and the alternative was shooting the channel. Ken got out upon the rocks, only to find that drifting the boat round the sharp point was out of the question, owing to a dangerously swift current. Ken tried the depth of the water—about four feet. Then he dragged the boat back a little distance and stepped into the river.

"Look! Look!" cried Pepe, pointing to the bank.

About ten yards away was a bare shelf of mud glistening with water and showing the deep tracks of a crocodile. It was a slide, and manifestly had just been vacated. The crocodile-tracks resembled the imprints of a giant's hand.

"Come out!" yelled George, and Pepe jabbered to his saints.

"We've got to go down this river," Ken replied, and he kept on wading till he got the boat in the current. He was frightened, of course, but he kept on despite that. The boat lurched into the channel, stern first, and he leaped up on the bow. It shot down with the speed of a toboggan, and the boat whirled before he could scramble to the oars. What was worse, an overhanging tree with dead snags left scarce room to pass beneath.

Ken ducked to prevent being swept overboard, and one of the snags that brushed and scraped him ran under his belt and lifted him into the air. He grasped at the first thing he could lay hands on, which happened to be a box, but he could not hold to it because the boat threatened to go on, leaving him kicking in midair and holding up a box of potatoes. Ken clutched a gunwale, only to see the water swell dangerously over the edge. In angry helplessness he loosened his hold. Then the snag broke, just in the nick of time, for in a second more the boat would have been swept away. Ken fell across the bow, held on, and soon drifted from under the threshing branches, and seized the oars.

Pepe and George and Hal walked round the ledge and, even when they reached Ken, had not stopped laughing.

"Boys, it wasn't funny," declared Ken, soberly.

"I said it was coming to us," replied George.

There were rapids below, and Ken went at them with stern eyes and set lips. It was the look of men who face obstacles in getting out of the wilderness. More than one high wave circled spitefully round Pepe's broad shoulders.

They came to a fall where the river dropped a few feet straight down. Ken sent the boys below. Hal and George made a detour. But Pepe jumped off the ledge into shallow water.

"Ah-h!" yelled Pepe.

Ken was becoming accustomed to Pepe's wild yell, but there was a note in this which sent a shiver over him. Pepe appeared to be sailing out into the pool. But his feet were not moving.

Ken had only an instant, but in that he saw under Pepe a long, yellow, swimming shape, leaving a wake in the water. Pepe had jumped upon the back of a crocodile. He seemed paralyzed, or else he was wisely trusting himself there rather than in the water. Ken was too shocked to offer advice. Indeed, he would not have known how to meet this situation.

Suddenly Pepe leaped for a dry stone, and the energy of his leap carried him into the river beyond. Like a flash he was out again, spouting water.

"Guess this'll be crocodile day," said Ken, "Boys, look out below."

Ken shoved the boat over the ledge in line with Pepe, and it floated to him, while Ken picked his way round the rocky shore. The boys piled aboard again. The day began to get hot. Ken cautioned the boys to avoid wading, if possible, and to be extremely careful where they stepped. Pepe pointed now and then to huge bubbles breaking on the surface of the water and said they were made by crocodiles.

From then on Ken's hands were full. He struck swift water, where rapid after rapid, fall on fall, took the boat downhill at a rate to afford him satisfaction. The current had a five or six mile speed, and, as Ken had no portages to make and the corrugated rapids of big waves gave him speed, he made by far the best time of the voyage.

The hot hours passed—cool for the boys because they were always wet. The sun sank behind a hill. The wind ceased to whip the streamers of moss. At last, in a gathering twilight, Ken halted at a wide, flat rock to make camp.

"Forty miles today if we made an inch!" exclaimed Ken.

The boys said more.

They built a fire, cooked supper, and then rolled into their blankets.

Romer's Turkeys

Tales of Lonely Trails (1922)

ROMER AND THE TURKEYS

From "Tonto Basin" in *Tales of Lonely Trails* (1922)

Romer Grey is on his first hunt with his father, Zane Grey, and Uncle R.C. Are they smarter than the turkeys or will the big birds get away? This story is part of a book about Zane Grey's adventures in the American West called Tales of Lonely Trails *you might enjoy.*

The sun was high and hot when we rode off. The pleasant and dusty stretches alternated. About one o'clock we halted on the edge of a deep wooded ravine to take our usual noonday rest. I scouted along the edge in the hope of seeing game of some kind.

Presently I heard the cluck-cluck of turkeys. Slipping along to an open place I peered down to be thrilled by sight of four good-sized turkeys. They were walking along the open strip of dry stream-bed at the bottom of the ravine. One was chasing grasshoppers. They were fairly close. I took aim at one, and thought I could have hit him, but suddenly I remembered Romer and R.C. So I slipped back and called them.

Hurriedly and stealthily we returned to the point where I had seen the turkeys. Romer had a pale face and wonderfully bright eyes; his actions resembled those of a stalking Indian. The turkeys were farther down, but still in plain sight. I told R.C. to take the boy and slip down, and run and hide and run till they got close enough for a shot. I would keep to the edge of the ravine.

Some moments later I saw R.C. and the boy running and stooping and creeping along the bottom of the ravine. Then I ran myself to reach a point opposite the turkeys, so in case they flew uphill I might get a shot. But I did not see them, and nothing happened. I lost sight of the turkeys.

R.C. and Romer came wagging up the hill, both red and wet and tired. R.C. carried a small turkey, about the size of a chicken. He told me, between pants, that they chased the four large turkeys, and were young ones. They ran every way. He got one. Then he told me, between more pants and some laughs, that Romer had chased the little turkeys all over the ravine, almost catching several.

Romer said for himself: "I just almost pulled feathers out of their tails. Gee! if I'd had a gun!"

After we had unpacked and while the men were pitching the tents and getting supper I took Romer on a hunt up the creek. I was considerably pleased to see good-sized trout in the deeper pools. A little way above camp the creek forked. As the right-hand branch appeared to be larger and more attractive we followed its course. Soon the bustle of camp life and the sound of the horses were left far behind. Romer slipped along beside me stealthily as an Indian, all eyes and ears.

We had not traveled thus for a quarter of a mile when my quick ear caught the cluck-cluck of turkeys. "Listen," I whispered, halting. Romer became like a statue, his dark eyes dilating, his nostrils quivering, his whole body strung. He was a Zane all right. A turkey called again; then another answered. Romer started, and nodded his head vehemently.

"Come on now, right behind me," I whispered. "Step where I step and do what I do. Don't break any twigs."

Cautiously we glided up the creek, listening now and then to get the direction, until we came to an open place where we could see some distance up a ridge. The turkey clucks came from across the creek somewhere up this open aisle of the forest. I crawled ahead several rods to a more advantageous point, much pleased to note that Romer kept noiselessly at my heels. Then from behind a stone we peeped out. Almost at once a turkey flew down from a tree into the open lane.

"Look Dad!" whispered Romer, wildly. I had to hold him down.

"That's a hen turkey," I said. "See, it's small and dull-colored. The gobblers are big, shiny, and they have red on their heads."

made out grapevines, and I saw several animated dark patches among them. As I looked three turkeys flopped down to the ground. One was a gobbler of considerable size, with beautiful white and bronze feathers. Rather suspiciously he looked down our way.

The distance was not more than a hundred yards. I aimed at him, feeling as I did so how Romer quivered beside me, but I had no confidence in Copple's rifle. The sights were wrong for me. The stock did not fit me. So, hoping for a closer and better shot, I let this opportunity pass. Of course I should have taken it.

The gobbler clucked and began to trot up the ridge, with the others after him. They were not frightened, but they appeared rather suspicious. When they disappeared in the woods Romer and I got up, and hurried in pursuit.

"Gee! Why didn't you peg that gobbler?" broke out Romer, breathlessly. "Wasn't he a peach?"

When we reached the top of the ridge we advanced very cautiously again. Another open place led to a steep, rocky hillside with cedars and pines growing somewhat separated. I was disappointed in not seeing the turkeys. Then in our anxiety and eagerness we hurried on, not noiselessly by any means.

All of a sudden there was a rustle, and then a great whir of wings. Three turkeys flew like grouse away into the woods. Next I saw the white gobbler running up the rocky hillside. At first he was in the open. Aiming as best I could I waited for him to stop or hesitate. But he did neither.

"Peg him, Dad!" yelled Romer.

The lad was right. My best chance I had again forfeited. To hit a running wild turkey with a rifle bullet was a feat I had not done so often as to inspire conceit. The gobbler was wise, too. For that matter all grown gobblers are as wise as old bucks, except in the spring mating season, when it is a crime to hunt them. This one, just as I got a bead on him, always ran behind a rock or tree or shrub. Finally in desperation I took a snap shot at him, hitting under him, had the satisfaction of seeing where my bullets struck up the dust, even though they did go wide of the mark. After my last shot the gobbler disappeared.

"Well, Dad, you sure throwed the dirt over him!" declared Romer.

"Son, I don't believe I could hit a flock of barns with this gun," I replied, gazing doubtfully at the old, shiny, wire-wrapped, worn-out Winchester Copple had lent me. I had been told that he was a fine marksman and could drive a nail with it.

Upon my return to camp I tried out the rifle, carefully, with a rest, to find that it was not accurate. Moreover it did not throw the bullets consistently. It shot high, wide, low; and right there I abandoned any further use for it. R.C. tried to make me take his rifle to use on the hunting trip; Nielsen and Lee wanted me to take theirs, but I was disgusted with myself and refused.

"Thanks, boys," I said. "Maybe this will be a lesson to me."

After supper this evening R.C. heard a turkey call up on the hill east of camp. Then I heard it, and Romer also. We ran out a ways into the open to listen the better. R.C.'s ears were exceptionally keen. He could hear a squirrel jump a long distance in the forest. In this case he distinctly heard three turkeys fly up into trees. I heard one. Romer declared he heard a flock.

Then R.C. located a big bronze and white gobbler on a lower limb of a huge pine. Presently I too espied it. Whereupon we took shot-gun and rifle, and sallied forth sure of fetching back to camp some wild turkey meat. Romer tagged at our heels.

Hurrying to the slope we climbed up at least three-quarters of the way, as swiftly as possible. And that was work enough to make me wet and hot. The sun had set and twilight was upon us, so that we needs must hurry if we were to be successful.

Locating the big gobbler turned out to be a task. We had to climb over brush and around rocks, up a steep slope, rather open; and we had to do it without being seen or making noise. Romer, despite his

At last I espied our quarry, and indeed the sight was thrilling. Wild turkey gobblers to me, who had hunted them enough to learn how sagacious and cunning and difficult to stalk they were, always seemed as provocative of excitement as larger game. This big fellow hopped up from limb to limb of the huge dead pine, and he bobbed around as if undecided, and tried each limb for a place to roost. Then he hopped farther up until we lost sight of him in the gnarled net-work of branches.

R.C. wanted me to slip on alone, but I preferred to have him and Romer go too. So we slipped stealthily upward until we reached the level. Then progress was easier. I went to the left with the rifle, and R.C. with the .20-gauge, and Romer, went around to the right.

How rapidly it was growing dark! Low down in the forest I could not distinguish objects. We circled that big pine tree, and I made rather a wide detour, perhaps eighty yards from it. At last I got the upper part of the dead pine silhouetted against the western sky. Moving to and fro I finally made out a large black lump way out upon a spreading branch. Could that be the gobbler?

I studied that dark enlarged part of the limb with great intentness, and I had about decided that it was only a knot when I saw a long neck shoot out. That lump was the wise old turkey all right. He was almost in the top of the tree and far out from the trunk. No wild cat or lynx could ever surprise him there! I reflected upon the instinct that governed him to protect his life so cunningly. Safe he was from all but man and gun!

When I came to aim at him with the rifle I found that I could see only a blur of sights. Other branches and the tip of a very high pine adjoining made a dark background. I changed my position, working around to where the background was all open sky. It proved to be better. By putting the sights against this open sky I could faintly see the front sight through the blurred ring. It was a good long shot even for daylight, and I had a rifle I knew nothing about. But all the difficulty only made a keener zest.

Just then I heard Romer cry out excitedly, and then R.C. spoke under their feet. The gobbler grew uneasy. How he stretched out his long neck! He heard them below.

I called out low and sharp: "Stand still! Be quiet!"

Then I looked again through the blurred peep-sight until I caught the front sight against the open sky. This done I moved the rifle over until I had the sight aligned against the dark shape. Straining my eyes I held hard—then fired. The big dark lump on the branch changed shape, and fell, to alight with a sounding thump.

I heard Romer running, but could not see him. Then his high voice pealed out: "I got him, Dad. You made a grand peg!"

Not only had Romer gotten him, but he insisted on packing him back to camp. The gobbler was the largest I ever killed, not indeed one of the huge thirty-five pounders, but a fat, heavy turkey, and quite a load for a boy. Romer packed him down that steep slope in the dark without a slip, for which performance I allowed him to stay up a while around the camp-fire.

Zane Grey in His Baseball Uniform
Upper Delaware Scenic and Recreational River,
National Park Service, Zane Grey Museum.

THE WINNING BALL

Popular Magazine, May 1, 1910

In addition to being a great author and adventurer, Zane Great played semi-professional baseball in the years leading up to 1900. The game was much different then. Baseball diamonds were often uneven with little hills in the outfield. Local teams travelled the countryside looking to make money playing other teams. Some players didn't even use baseball gloves. In this short story, Zane Grey tells what happened when a "rabbit" got into a game. If you like this story, you should read The Red Headed Outfield, *one of Zane Grey's books about the game back when he was a ballplayer.*

One day in July our Rochester club, leader in the Eastern League, had returned to the hotel after winning a double-header from the Syracuse club. For some occult reason there was to be a lay-off next day and then on the following another double-header. These double-headers we hated next to exhibition games. Still a lay-off for twenty-four hours, at that stage of the race, was a Godsend, and we received the news with exclamations of pleasure.

After dinner we were all sitting in front of the hotel when our manager, Merritt, came hurriedly out of the lobby. It struck me that he appeared a little flustered.

"Say, you fellars," he said brusquely. "Pack your suits and be ready for the bus at seven-thirty."

For a moment there was a blank, ominous silence, while we assimilated the meaning of his terse speech.

"I've got a good thing on for tomorrow," continued the manager. "Sixty per cent gate receipts if we win. That Guelph team is hot stuff, though."

"Guelph!" exclaimed some of the players suspiciously. "Where's Guelph?"

"It's in Canada. We'll take the night express an' get there tomorrow in time for the game. An' we'll hev to hustle."

Upon Merritt then rained a multiplicity of excuses. Gillinger was not well, and ought to have that day's rest. Snead's eyes would profit by a lay-off. Deerfoot Browning was leading the league in base running, and as his legs were all bruised and scraped by sliding, a manager who was not an idiot would have a care of such valuable runmakers for his team. Lake had a "Charley-horse." Hathaway's arm was sore. Bane's stomach threatened gastritis. Spike Doran's finger needed a chance to heal. I was stale, and the other players, three pitchers, swore their arms should be in the hospital.

"Cut it out!" said Merritt, getting exasperated. "You'd all lay down on me—now, wouldn't you? Well, listen to this: McDougal pitched today; he doesn't go. Blake works Friday, he doesn't go. But the rest of you puffed-up, high-salaried stiffs pack your grips quick. See? It'll cost any fresh fellar fifty for missin' the train."

So that was how eleven of the Rochester team found themselves moodily boarding a Pullman en route for Buffalo and Canada. We went to bed early and arose late.

Guelph lay somewhere in the interior of Canada, and we did not expect to get there until 1 o'clock.

As it turned out, the train was late; we had to dress hurriedly in the back room, pack our citizen clothes in our grips and leave the train to go direct to the ball grounds without time for lunch.

It was a tired, dusty-eyed, peevish crowd of ball players that climbed into a waiting bus at the little station.

We had never heard of Guelph; we did not care anything about rube baseball teams. Baseball was not play to us; it was the hardest kind of work, and of all things an exhibition game was an abomination.

The Guelph players, strapping lads, met us with every mark of respect and courtesy and escorted us to the field with a brass band that was loud in welcome, if not harmonious in tune.

Some 500 men and boys trotted curiously along with us, for all the world as if the bus were a circus parade cage filled with striped tigers. What a rustic, motley crowd massed about in and on that ball ground. There must have been 10,000.

The audience was strange to us. The Indians, half-breeds, French-Canadians; the huge, hulking, bearded farmers or traders, or trappers, whatever they were, were new to our baseball experience.

The players themselves, however, earned the largest share of our attention. By the time they had practiced a few moments we looked at Merritt and Merritt looked at us.

These long, powerful, big-handed lads evidently did not know the difference between lacrosse and baseball; but they were quick as cats on their feet, and they scooped up the ball in a way wonderful to see. And throw!—it made a professional's heart swell just to see them line the ball across the diamond.

"Lord! What whips these lads have!" exclaimed Merritt. "Hope we're not up against it. If this team should beat us we wouldn't draw a handful at Toronto. We can't afford to be beaten. Jump around and cinch the game quick. If we get in a bad place, I'll sneak in the `rabbit.' "

The "rabbit" was a baseball similar in appearance to the ordinary league ball; under its horse-hide cover, however, it was remarkably different.

An ingenious fan, a friend of Merritt, had removed the covers from a number of league balls and sewed them on rubber balls of his own making. They could not be distinguished from the regular article, not even by an experienced professional—until they were hit. Then! The fact that after every bounce one of these rubber balls bounded swifter and higher had given it the name of the "rabbit."

Many a game had the "rabbit" won for us at critical stages. Of course it was against the rules of the league, and of course every player in the league knew about it; still, when it was judiciously and cleverly brought into a close game, the "rabbit" would be in play, and very probably over the fence, before the opposing captain could learn of it, let alone appeal to the umpire.

"Fellars, look at that guy who's goin' to pitch," suddenly spoke up one of the team.

Many as were the country players whom we seasoned and traveled professionals had run across, this twirler outclassed them for remarkable appearance. Moreover, what put an entirely different tinge to our momentary humor was the discovery that he was as wild as a March hare and could throw a ball so fast that it resembled a pea shot from a boy's air gun.

Deerfoot led our batting list, and after the first pitched ball, which he did not see, and the second, which ticked his shirt as it shot past, he turned to us with an expression that made us groan inwardly.

When Deerfoot looked that way it meant the pitcher was dangerous. Deerfoot made no effort to swing at the next ball, and was promptly called out on strikes.

I was second at bat, and went up with some reluctance. I happened to be leading the league in both long distance and safe hitting, and I doted on speed. But having stopped many mean in-shoots with various parts of my anatomy, I was rather squeamish about facing backwoods yaps who had no control.

When I had watched a couple of his pitches, which the umpire called strikes, I gave him credit for as much speed as Rusie. These balls were as straight as a string, singularly without curve, jump, or variation of any kind. I lined the next one so hard at the shortstop that it cracked like a pistol as it struck his hands and whirled him half off his feet. Still he hung to the ball and gave opportunity for the first crash of applause.

"Boys, he's a trifle wild," I said to my team-mates, "but he has the most beautiful ball to hit you ever saw. I don't believe he uses a curve, and when we once time that speed we'll kill it."

Next inning, after old man Hathaway had baffled the Canadians with his wide, tantalizing curves, my predictions began to be verified. Snead rapped one high and far to deep right field. To our infinite surprise, however, the right fielder ran with fleetness that made our own Deerfoot seem slow, and he got under the ball and caught it.

Doran sent a sizzling grasscutter down toward left. The lanky third baseman darted over, dived down, and, coming up with the ball, exhibited the power of a throwing arm that made us all green with envy.

Then, when the catcher chased a foul fly somewhere back in the crowd and caught it, we began to take notice.

"Lucky stabs!" said Merritt cheerfully. "They can't keep that up. We'll drive him to the woods next time."

But they did keep it up; moreover, they became more brilliant as the game progressed. What with Hathaway's heady pitching we soon disposed of them when at the bat; our turns, however, owing to the wonderful fielding of these backwoodsmen, were also fruitless.

Merritt, with his mind ever on the slice of gate money coming if we won, began to fidget and fume and find fault.

"You're a swell lot of champions, now, ain't you?" he observed between innings.

All baseball players like to bat, and nothing pleases them so much as base hits; on the other hand, nothing is quite so painful as to send out hard liners only to see them caught. And it seemed as if every man on our team connected with that lanky twirler's fast high ball and hit with the force that made the bat spring only to have one of these rubes get his big hands upon it.

Considering that we were in no angelic frame of mind before the game started, and in view of Merritt's persistently increasing ill humor, this failure of ours to hit a ball safely gradually worked us into a kind of frenzy. From indifference we passed to determination, and from that to sheer passionate purpose.

Luck appeared to be turning in the sixth inning. With one out, Lake hit a beauty to right. Doran beat an infield grounder and reached first. Hathaway struck out.

With Browning up and me next, the situation looked rather precarious for the Canadians.

"Say, Deerfoot," whispered Merritt, "dump one down the third-base line. He's playin' deep. It's a pipe. Then the bases will be full an' Reddy'll clean up."

In a stage like that Browning was a man absolutely to depend upon. He placed a slow bunt in the grass toward third and sprinted for first. The third baseman fielded the ball, but, being confused, did not know where to throw it.

"Stick it in your basket," yelled Merritt, in a delight that showed how hard he was pulling for the gate money, and his beaming smile as he turned to me was inspiring. "Now, Reddy, it's up to you! I'm not worrying about what's happened so far. I know, with you at bat in a pinch, it's all off!"

Merritt's compliment was pleasing, but it did not augment my purpose, for that already had reached the highest mark. Love of hitting, if no other thing, gave me the thrilling fire to arise to the opportunity. Selecting my light bat, I went up and faced the rustic twirler and softly said things to him.

He delivered the ball, and I could have yelled aloud, so fast, so straight, so true it sped toward me. Then I hit it harder than I had ever hit a ball in my life. The bat sprung, as if it were whalebone. And the ball took a bullet course between center and left. So beautiful a hit was it that I watched as I ran.

Out of the tail of my eye I saw the center fielder running. When I rounded first base I got a good look at this fielder, and though I had seen the greatest outfielders the game ever produced, I never saw one that covered ground so swiftly as he.

On the ball soared, and began to drop; on the fielder sped, and began to disappear over a little hill back of his position. Then he reached up with a long arm and marvelously caught the ball in one hand. He went out of sight as I touched second base, and the heterogeneous crowd knew about a great play to make more noise than a herd of charging buffalo.

In the next half inning our opponents, by clean drives, scored two runs and we in our turn again went out ignominiously. When the first of the eighth came we were desperate and clamored for the "rabbit."

"I've sneaked it in," said Merritt, with a low voice. "Got it to the umpire on the last passed ball. See, the pitcher's got it now. Boys, it's all off but the fireworks! Now, break loose!"

A peculiarity about the "rabbit" was the fact that though it felt as light as the regulation league ball it could not be thrown with the same speed and to curve it was an impossibility.

Bane hit the first delivery from our Hoosier stumbling block. The ball struck the ground and began to bound toward short. With every bound it went swifter, longer and higher, and it bounced clear over the shortstop's head. Lake chopped one in front of the plate, and it rebounded from the ground straight up so high that both runners were safe before it came down.

Doran hit to the pitcher. The ball caromed his leg, scooted fiendishly at the second baseman, and tried to run up all over him like a tame squirrel. Bases full!

Hathaway got a safe fly over the infield and two runs tallied. The pitcher, in spite of the help of the umpire, could not locate the plate for Balknap, and gave him a base on balls. Bases full again!

Deerfoot slammed a hot liner straight at the second baseman, which, striking squarely in his hands, recoiled as sharply as if it had struck a wall. Doran scored, and still the bases were filled.

The laboring pitcher began to get rattled; he could not find his usual speed; he knew it, but evidently could not account for it.

When I came to bat, indications were not wanting that the Canadian team would soon be up in the air. The long pitcher delivered the "rabbit," and got it low down by my knees, which was an unfortunate thing for him. I swung on that one, and trotted round the bases behind the runners while the center and left fielders chased the ball.

Gillinger weighed nearly two hundred pounds, and he got all his weight under the "rabbit." It went so high that we could scarcely see it. All the infielders rushed in, and after staggering around, with heads bent back, one of them, the shortstop, managed to get under it.

The "rabbit" bounded forty feet out of his hands!

When Snead's grounder nearly tore the third baseman's leg off; when Bane's hit proved as elusive as a flitting shadow; when Lake's liner knocked the pitcher flat, and Doran's fly leaped high out of the center fielder's glove—then those earnest, simple, country ballplayers realized something was wrong. But they imagined it was in themselves, and after a short spell of rattles, they steadied up and tried harder than ever. The motions they went through trying to stop that jumping jackrabbit of a ball were ludicrous in the extreme.

Finally, through a foul, a short fly, and a scratch hit to first, they retired the side and we went into the field with the score 14 to 2 in our favor.

But Merritt had not found it possible to get the "rabbit" out of play!

We spent a fatefully anxious few moments squabbling with the umpire and captain over the "rabbit." At the idea of letting those herculean railsplitters have a chance to hit the rubber ball we felt our blood run cold.

"But this ball has a rip in it," blustered Gillinger. He lied atrociously. A microscope could not have discovered as much as a scratch in that smooth leather.

"Sure it has," supplemented Merritt, in the suave tones of a stage villain. "We're used to playing with good balls."

"Why did you ring this one in on us?" asked the captain. "We never threw out this ball. We want a chance to hit it."

That was just the one thing we did not want them to have. But fate played against us.

"Get up on your toes, now an' dust," said Merritt. "Take your medicine, you lazy sit-in-front-of-the-hotel stiffs! Think of pay day!"

Not improbably we all entertained the identical thought that old man Hathaway was the last pitcher under the sun calculated to be effective with the "rabbit." He never relied on speed; in fact, Merritt often scornfully accused him of being unable to break a pane of glass; he used principally what we called floaters and a change of pace. Both styles were absolutely impractical with the "rabbit."

"It's comin' to us, all right, all right!" yelled Deerfoot to me, across the intervening grass. I was of the opinion that it did not take any genius to make Deerfoot's ominous prophecy.

Old man Hathaway gazed at Merritt on the bench as if he wished the manager could hear what he was calling him and then at his fellow players as if both to warn and beseech them. Then he pitched the "rabbit."

Crack!

The big lumbering Canadian rapped the ball at Crab Bane. I did not see it, because it went so fast, but I gathered from Crab's actions that it must have been hit in his direction. At any rate, one of his legs flopped out sidewise as if it had been suddenly jerked, and he fell in a heap. The ball, a veritable "rabbit" in its wild jumps, headed on for Deerfoot, who contrived to stop it with his knees.

The next batter resembled the first one, and the hit likewise, only it leaped wickedly at Doran and went through his hands as if they had been paper. The third man batted up a very high fly to Gillinger. He clutched at it with his huge shovel hands, but he could not hold it. The way he pounced upon the ball, dug it out of the grass, and hurled it at Hathaway, showed his anger.

Obviously Hathaway had to stop the throw, for he could not get out of the road, and he spoke to his captain in what I knew were no complimentary terms.

Thus began retribution. Those husky lads continued to hammer the "rabbit" at the infielders and as it bounced harder at every bounce so they batted harder at every bat.

Another singular feature about the "rabbit" was the seeming impossibility for professionals to hold it. Their familiarity with it, their understanding of its vagaries and inconsistencies, their mortal dread made fielding it a much more difficult thing than for their opponents.

By way of variety, the lambasting Canadians commenced to lambast a few over the hills and far away, which chased Deerfoot and me until our tongues lolled out.

Every time a run crossed the plate the motley crowd howled, roared, danced and threw up their hats. The members of the batting team pranced up and down the side lines, giving a splendid imitation of cannibals celebrating the occasion of a feast.

Once Snead stooped down to trap the "rabbit," and it slipped through his legs, for which his comrades jeered him unmercifully. Then a brawny batter sent up a tremendously high fly between short and third.

"You take it!" yelled Gillinger to Bane.

"You take it!" replied the Crab, and actually walked backward. That ball went a mile high. The sky was hazy, gray, the most perplexing in which to judge a fly ball. An ordinary fly gave trouble enough in the gauging.

Gillinger wandered around under the ball for what seemed an age. It dropped as swiftly as a rocket shoots upward. Gillinger went forward in a circle, then sidestepped, and threw up his broad hands. He misjudged the ball, and it hit him fairly on the head and bounced almost to where Doran stood at second.

Our big captain wilted. Time was called. But Gillinger, when he came to, refused to leave the game and went back to third with a lump on his head as large as a goose egg.

Every one of his teammates was sorry, yet every one howled in glee. To be hit on the head was the unpardonable sin for a professional.

Old man Hathaway gradually lost what little speed he had, and with it his nerve. Every time he pitched the "rabbit" he dodged. That was about the funniest and strangest thing ever seen on a ball field. Yet it had an element of tragedy.

Hathaway's expert contortions saved his head and body on divers occasions, but presently a low bounder glanced off the grass and manifested an affinity for his leg.

We all knew from the crack and the way the pitcher went down that the "rabbit" had put him out of the game. The umpire called time, and Merritt came running on the diamond.

"Hard luck, old man," said the manager. "That'll make a green and yellow spot all right. Boys, we're still two runs to the good. There's one out, an' we can win yet. Deerfoot, you're as badly crippled as Hathaway. The bench for you. Hooker will go to center, an' I'll pitch."

Merritt's idea did not strike us as a bad one. He could pitch, and he always kept his arm in prime condition. We welcomed him into the fray for two reasons—because he might win the game, and because he might be overtaken by the baseball Nemesis.

While Merritt was putting on Hathaway's baseball shoes, some of us endeavored to get the "rabbit" away from the umpire, but he was too wise.

Merritt received the innocent-looking ball with a look of mingled disgust and fear, and he summarily ordered us to our positions.

Not far had we gone, however, when we were electrified by the umpire's sharp words:

"Naw! Naw, you don't. I saw you change the ball I gave you fer one in your pocket! Naw! You don't come enny of your American dodges on us! Gimmee thet ball, an' you use the other, or I'll stop the game."

Wherewith the shrewd umpire took the ball from Merritt's hand and fished the "rabbit" from his pocket. Our thwarted manager stuttered his wrath. "Y-you be-be-wh-whiskered y-yap! I'll g-g-give—"

What dire threat he had in mind never materialized, for he became speechless. He glowered upon the cool little umpire, and then turned grandly toward the plate.

It may have been imagination, yet I made sure Merritt seemed to shrink and grow smaller before he pitched a ball. For one thing the plate was uphill from the pitcher's box, and then the fellow standing there loomed up like a hill and swung a bat that would have served as a wagon tongue. No wonder Merritt evinced nervousness. Presently he whirled and delivered the ball.

Bing!

A dark streak and a white puff of dust over second base showed how safe that hit was. By dint of manful body work, Hooker contrived to stop the "rabbit" in mid-center. Another run scored. Human nature was proof against this temptation, and Merritt's players tendered him manifold congratulations and dissertations.

"Grand, you old skinflint, grand!"

"There was a two-dollar bill stickin' on thet hit. Why didn't you stop it?"

"Say, Merritt, what little brains you've got will presently be ridin' on the rabbit.' "

"You will chase up these exhibition games!"

"Take your medicine now. Ha! Ha! Ha!"

After these merciless taunts, and particularly after the next slashing hit that tied the score, Merritt looked appreciably smaller and humbler. He threw up another ball, and actually shied as it neared the plate. The giant who was waiting to slug it evidently thought better of his eagerness as far as that pitch was concerned, for he let it go by. Merritt got the next ball higher. With a mighty swing, the batsman hit a terrific liner right at the pitcher.

Quick as lightning, Merritt wheeled, and the ball struck him with the sound of two boards brought heavily together with a smack. Merritt did not fall; he melted to the ground and writhed while the runners scored with more tallies than they needed to win.

What did we care! Justice had been done us, and we were unutterably happy. Crab Bane stood on his head; Gillinger began a war dance; old man Hathaway hobbled out to the side lines and whooped like an Indian; Snead rolled over and over in the grass. All of us broke out into typical expressions of baseball frenzy, and individual ones illustrating our particular moods.

Merritt got up and made a dive for the ball. With face positively flaming he flung it far beyond the merry crowd, over into a swamp. Then he limped for the bench. Which throw ended the most memorable game ever recorded to the credit of the "rabbit."

APPENDICES

Notes

Zane Grey: Author and Adventurer

Discussion Guide for Teachers
and Reading Group Leaders

Zane Grey Museums

List of Zane Grey Works

Invitation to Join Zane Grey's West Society

NOTES

All of the stories in *The Zane Grey Primer* are either in the public domain and/or available through fair use privilege. The editors acknowledge the original source of the stories and the wisdom and contributions of Zane Grey, Inc. in protecting the integrity of Zane Grey's works through the years. These sources include:

"Ken and Hal Meet The Mountain Lions" is condensed from a chapter in *The Young Lion Hunter* published in 1911.

"Old Muddy Miser" is condensed from a chapter in "The Living Past," as published in the December 1986 edition of the *Zane Grey Reporter.*

"Lightning" was published in *Outing Magazine* in April 1910.

"Monty Price's Nightingale" was published in *The Popular Magazine* on May 7, 1915.

"The Lord of Lackawaxen Creek" was published in *Outing Magazine* in May 1909.

"Crocodile Day" was condensed from *Ken Ward in the Jungle,* published in 1912.

"Romer and the Turkeys" was condensed from the chapter entitled "Tonto Rim" in the book *Tales of Lonely Trails* published in 1922.

"The Winning Ball" was published in *Popular Magazine* on May 1, 1910.

ZANE GREY:
AUTHOR AND ADVENTURER

Born in Zanesville, OH, in 1872, Zane Grey was the great-grandson of Colonel Ebenezer Zane, founder of Fort Henry (now Wheeling, WV). An avid reader, athlete, fisherman and outdoorsman, Grey attended the University of Pennsylvania on a baseball scholarship, earned a degree in dentistry and opened a dental office in New York City. He later admitted he only settled there because "that's where the publishers were."

Zane Grey had always wanted to be a writer. His first book *Betty Zane*, self-published in 1903, was the heroic tale of his own Zane ancestors. Then in 1907, he met Buffalo Jones, who invited him to go to Arizona. He went—and fell under the spell of the West. For the next 30 years, Grey traveled the West, compiling the descriptions and stories that would become the hallmarks of his writing. It was Grey who popularized the concept of "The Old West," spawning the wave of Western books and films that followed.

Beginning in 1908, Zane Grey's books were published almost every year for a half century; and at least one of his books appeared in the top ten for all but two years between 1915 and 1924. At one time, his books outsold all others except the Bible and the McGuffey Readers. Now in more than 20 languages, most of Grey's works are still in print. The 110-130 films adapted from his stories launched the careers of Hollywood stars like John Wayne and Gary Cooper. Despite the critics, who often savaged his work, Grey was one of the world's first millionaire authors.

In addition to his role as the father of the Western romance novel, Grey was known worldwide as the greatest fisherman of his time and a dedicated outdoorsman. In his collection of the author's outdoor adventures entitled *Zane Grey—Outdoorsman*, George Reiger summarizes Grey's love of nature and contributions as one of America's environmental pioneers.

Zane Grey's writings are in effect diaries immortalizing a rugged outdoor landscape that, even as he wrote, was changing, fading. Working against time like a painter hoping to fix an impression of a particular sunset, Zane Grey wrote for all us who will never see an undammed Rogue River or an undeveloped Florida Keys.

Zane Grey is our contemporary. In his campaigns against the overgrazing of rangeland and the reckless cutting of timber, in his condemnation of the noise and exhausts of automobiles, in predictions that indiscriminate netting would dangerously deplete certain fishes even in the so-called limitless seas, Zane Grey was ahead of his time.

—George Reiger, *Zane Grey: Outdoorsman,* vii-viii

When he died of a heart attack in Altadena, CA, in 1939, he left his wife Dolly, three children and loyal readers worldwide to mourn his passing. Happily, Zane Grey and his love for the West have not been forgotten. In 2012, Zane Grey's West Society published the *Centennial Edition* of Grey's most renowned Western classic, *Riders of the Purple Sage.* The same year, the Library of Congress selected the novel as one of the "100 Books that Shaped America."

DISCUSSION GUIDE
FOR TEACHERS AND
READING GROUP LEADERS

1. Zane Grey wrote before television was invented. He spends time describing wild places and animals in detail so the reader can imagine what is happening. What was your favorite wild place or animal in these stories?

2. Many of Zane Grey's stories are over 100 years old. In those days, young people entertained themselves differently from today. Tell us about one activity described in these stories that you have actually done.

3. Would these stories make good movies? If so, what current-day actor would you choose to play the hero and why? Don't forget that young women can be heroes, too.

4. These stories occurred in the outdoors. How would the stories be different if they took place near your town?

5. Tell us about a time in one of these stories when a character had to make a decision. Would you have made the same decision? Explain why or why not.

6. Zane Grey's stories are written in a different style from what you usually read today. What did you like about his way of telling stories? What didn't you like?

7. Which of these stories was your favorite? If the hero of that story was a modern superheroes, what would he or she have done differently?

ZANE GREY MUSEUMS

ZANE GREY MUSEUM
Lackawaxen, Pennsylvania

Zane and Dolly Grey's Lackawaxen home on the Delaware River is now a National Historic Site administered by the National Park Service. Grey and his wife, Dolly, are buried in Union Cemetery nearby.
Web: http://www.nps.gov/upde/historyculture/zanegrey.htm

ZANE GREY CABIN/RIM COUNTRY MUSEUM
Payson, Arizona
Museum of the natural and cultural history of the Payson area. Features a replica of Zane Grey's cabin under the Mogollon Rim in Payson. Operated by the Rim Country Museum.
Web: http://www.rimcountrymuseums.com/

NATIONAL ROAD & ZANE GREY MUSEUM
Norwich (Zanesville), Ohio
Museum tracing the history of the National Road and the role of Zane Grey's renowned ancestors in the settling of frontier Ohio. Features an extensive Zane Grey exhibit covering his early years, baseball career, dental practice, outdoor interests and world fishing records, as well as his writings and the 100+ films made from his stories.
Web: http://www.ohiohistory.org/museums-and-historic-sites/museum—historic-sites-by-name/national-road

ZANE GREY MUSEUM
Mormon Lake Lodge, Mormon Lake, Arizona
Museum features an array of Grey-related books, photographs, paintings, movie posters and much more. Unique exhibits include guns and many other artifacts and items owned or used by Zane Grey.
Web: http://www.mormonlakelodge.com/mormonlake/

LIST OF ZANE GREY WORKS

Zane Grey, one of the world's most prolific writers, holds a unique place in American literature. Best known for his stories of the American West, he also wrote historical fiction; works about fishing, baseball and world travel; and books for young readers. Grey's writings popularized the literary genre commonly known as the "Western."

Published during Grey's lifetime

Betty Zane (1903)
Spirit of the Border (1906)
The Last of the Plainsmen (1908)
The Last Trail (1909)
The Shortstop (1909)
The Heritage of the Desert (1910)*
The Young Forester (1910)*
The Young Pitcher (1911)
The Young Lion Hunter (1911)*
Riders of the Purple Sage (1912)*
Ken Ward in the Jungle (1912)
Desert Gold (1913)*
The Light of Western Stars (1914)*
The Lone Star Ranger (1915)*
The Rainbow Trail (1915)*
The Border Legion (1916)*
Wildfire (1917)*
The U.P. Trail (1918)*
The Desert of Wheat (1919)
Tales of Fishes (1919)
The Man of the Forest (1920)*
The Redheaded Outfield and Other Stories (1920)
The Mysterious Rider (1921)*
To the Last Man (1921)*
The Day of the Beast (1922)
Tales of Lonely Trails (1922)
Wanderer of the Wasteland (1923)*

Tappan's Burro (1923)*
Call of the Canyon (1924)*
Roping Lions in the Grand Canyon (1924)
Tales of Southern Rivers (1924)
The Thundering Herd (1925)*
The Vanishing American (1925)*
Tales of Fishing Virgin Seas (1925)
Under the Tonto Rim (1926)*
Tales of the Angler's Eldorado, New Zealand (1926)
Forlorn River (1927)*
Tales of Swordfish and Tuna (1927)
Nevada (1928)*
Wild Horse Mesa (1928)*
Don, the Story of a Dog (1928)*
Tales of Fresh Water Fishing (1928)
Fighting Caravans (1929)*
The Wolf Tracker (1930)*
The Shepherd of Guadaloupe (1930)*
Sunset Pass (1931)*
Tales of Tahitian Waters (1931)
Book of Camps and Trails (1931)
Arizona Ames (1932)*
Robbers Roost (1932)*
The Drift Fence (1933)*
The Hash Knife Outfit (1933)*
The Code of the West (1934)*
Thunder Mountain (1935)*
The Trail Driver (1935)*
The Lost Wagon Train (1936)*
West of the Pecos (1937)*
An American Angler in Australia (1937)
Raiders of Spanish Peaks (1938)*
Western Union (1939)*

Published posthumously

Knights of the Range (1939)*
30,000 on the Hoof (1940)*
Twin Sombreros (1940)*
Majesty's Rancho (1942)*
Omnibus (1943)
Stairs of Sand (1943)*
The Wilderness Trek (1944)
Shadow on the Trail (1946)*
Valley of Wild Horses (1947)*
Rogue River Feud (1948)
The Deer Stalker (1949)*
The Maverick Queen (1950)*
The Dude Ranger (1951)*
Captives of the Desert (1952)*
Adventures in Fishing (1952)
Wyoming (1953)*
Lost Pueblo (1954)*
Black Mesa (1955)*
Stranger from the Tonto (1956)*
The Fugitive Trail (1957)*
Arizona Clan (1958)*
Horse Heaven Hill (1959)*
The Ranger and Other Stories (1960)*
Blue Feather and Other Stories (1961)*
Boulder Dam (1963)
The Adventures of Finspot (1974)
The Reef Girl (1977)
The Westerner (1977)*
Tales from a Fisherman's Log (1978)
The Buffalo Hunter (1978)*
The Camp Robber and Other Stories (1979)*
The Lord of Lackawaxen Creek (1981)
The Last Ranger (1981)
George Washington, Frontiersman (1994)
The Rustlers of Pecos County (1995)*
Last of the Duanes (1996)*

Rangers of the Lone Star (1997)*
Woman of the Frontier (1998)*
The Great Trek: A Tale of Australia (1999)
Rangle River (2001)
Open Range (2002)*
The Desert Crucible (2003)*
Tonto Basin (2004)*
Top Hand (2004)*
Cabin Gulch (2006)*
Shower of Gold (2007)*
Tales of the Gladiator (2009)
Dorn of the Mountains (2009)*
Desert Heritage (2010)*
Buffalo Stampede (2011)*
War Comes to the Big Bend (2012)*
Silvermane (2013)*

*Western fiction

INVITATION TO JOIN
ZANE GREY'S WEST SOCIETY

After reading *The Zane Grey Primer,* we hope you'll want to read more of his books and learn more about Zane Grey, the author and person. One of the best ways to do this is to join Zane Grey's West Society. Our mission is "to promote interest in and knowledge of the eminent American author Zane Grey and his works." We are an international, non-profit, all-volunteer organization with members around the world—in Australia, New Zealand, England, Germany, Italy and France, as well as Canada and the US.

Annual member benefits include four issues of the *Zane Grey Review,* filled with articles about Grey, Society updates, member and meeting news and information for collectors and dealers. Another significant member benefit is access to the many collectors and experts in the Society, including some of the world's foremost authorities on Grey's life and works.

Membership also provides the opportunity to join us at our annual conventions, held in the exciting locales where Grey lived and traveled and wrote. During the convention, you will have a chance to discuss Grey with other enthusiasts, and to participate in the annual auction of collectible Zane Grey books and memorabilia. Each year Society members look forward to the convention and to spending time with other members of the extended "Zane Grey family."

For details about joining the Society or contact information, please visit our website:

www.zgws.org

To learn more about Zane Grey visit the
Zane Grey's West Society homepage at http://zgws.org or our
Facebook page at https://facebook.com/ZaneGreysWestSociety.